CONTENTS

THE SKIES OF THE MEDITERRANEAN AND NORTH AFRICA

THE SKIES OF THE PACIFIC

PREFACE

In World War I air power was a novelty rather than a serious military threat. Wooden and canvas biplanes twisted and turned like jousting knights of old in the skies above the wholesale slaughter of the ground war below. The Great War was a war of attrition, a war of hard-fought blood, sweat and tear-stained yards, a war of infantrymen and horses – a war of days gone by. Those who spoke of air power playing a decisive role in future wars were dismissed as dreamers.

A Memorable Milestone in the March of Man

Perceptions suddenly changed on 26 April 1937, during the Spanish Civil War. One of the first aerial terror bombing attacks on a civilian population was launched by Nazi Germany's Luftwaffe on the Basque town of Guernica in Northern Spain. With a population of 7,000 people, the town was almost entirely destroyed with a disputed number of civilian deaths thought to be anywhere between 400 and 800. Germany had demonstrated just what air supremacy could achieve in battle. The metal-framed monoplanes of the German Luftwaffe, with their liquid cooled engines and retractable landing gear, showed how far aircraft design had come since World War I. Top speeds had tripled; maximum altitudes had doubled and flight ranges and bomb payloads had increased enormously.

By 1945 jet fighters and rockets soared through the skies, and the war ended with US bombers dropping the world's first atomic weapons. This is the story of how air power came to decide the outcome of World War II. It is an extraordinary tale of great heroism and terrible suffering, from both the pilots in the air and the civilians on the ground. For the first time in history, warring nations looked not across at one another but up towards the skies.

The battles that were won and lost in the skies would become the single most important factor in determining which side won and which side lost the war. As Winston Churchill observed in 1949, the emergence of air power as the dominant force of war marked a turning point not just in the history of flight, or the history of warfare, but in the history of mankind.

Science ... placed novel and dangerous facilities in the hands of the most powerful countries. Humanity was informed that it could make machines that would fly through the air and vessels which could swim beneath the surface of the seas. The conquest of the air and the perfection of the art of flying fulfilled the dream which for thousands of years had glittered in human imagination. Certainly it was a marvellous and romantic event. Whether the bestowal of this gift upon an immature civilization composed of competing nations whose nationalism grew with every advance of democracy and who were as yet devoid of international organization, was a blessing or a curse has yet to be proved. On the whole I remain an optimist. For good or ill, air mastery is today the supreme expression of military power, and fleets and armies, however necessary, must accept a subordinate rank. This is a memorable milestone in the march of man.

Winston S. Churchill, 31 March 1949

(Right) World War II US Treasury poster.

THE RISE OF THE LUFTWAFFE

DATELINE ... I MARCH 1935 ... 30 SEPTEMBER 1939

On Adolf Hitler's orders, the Junkers Ju 52/3m had been hurriedly adapted and pressed into service as the Luftwaffe's first bomber. From these lowliest of beginnings, the Luftwaffe grew at an extraordinary rate. By 1935 it was possible for a complete fighter wing to participate in a fly-past on Hitler's birthday. By the following year, entire squadrons of the most modern military aircraft in the world flew low over the Führer's birthday parade. Soon Germany's air power had surpassed all the other European nations.

Invincible Air Squadrons

Just a few years earlier, the German Air Force didn't exist – at least not in any meaningful form. The Treaty of Versailles had decreed that, at the end of World War I, Germany's air force would be dismantled and only civilian aircraft allowed. There were just 140 aircraft left in the country, all of them commercial. Flying enthusiasts had to content themselves with gliders and, though the 1922 Treaty of Rapallo contained a secret clause that allowed Germany to conspire with the Soviet Union on aircraft development, the situation was largely unchanged by the time Hitler came to power in 1933. However six years later, on the eve of war, the Luftwaffe's Commander-in-Chief, Hermann Göring, who had been a fighter pilot in World War I, was buoyant.

> "... The Führer will not ask how big the bombers are ... only how many have we got ..."
>
> Hermann Göring

Since the 1st March, 1935, I and my colleagues, carrying out the Führer's intentions, had created at high speed the most modern air force which any nation could possess ... I am forever convinced that we cannot be conquered by force of arms. Fear of our invincible air squadrons and our ultra-modern, splendidly trained flak artillery has given many a hate-filled war-monger abroad bad dreams.

Reichsmarschall Hermann Göring
Commander-in-Chief, Luftwaffe, March 1935

Nazi leaders knew that tough battles lay ahead, but they were convinced that the Luftwaffe was equal to the task of conquering the combined might of the other European nations, even if the United States entered the war on their side. In the summer of 1939, the Luftwaffe had nine *Jagdgeschwader* (fighter wings), which were mostly equipped with Messerschmitt Bf 109s, four *Zerstörergeschwader* (destroyer wings) using the Messerschmitt Bf 110 fighter and 11 *Kampfgeschwader* (bomber wings) equipped with Heinkel He 111 and Dornier Do 17Z bombers. Four *Sturzkampfgeschwader* (dive bomber wings) completed the force, which numbered 373,000 personnel and 4,201 operational aircraft including 1,191 bombers, 361 dive bombers, 788 fighters, 431 heavy fighters and 488 transport planes.

A Conspicuous Absence

Missing from the Luftwaffe's array of aircraft was a long range heavy bomber. The Heinkel He 177 and Dornier Do 17 were light, twin-engined bombers that fulfilled Göring's requirement that bombers should be as fast – or faster – than fighters. Experience in the Spanish Civil War suggested that high level bombers had poor accuracy, and so dive-bombers were preferred whenever possible.

These excelled against small mobile targets, in support of a broader 'Blitzkrieg', but were not designed to travel large distances with vast payloads, being tactical rather than strategic bombers. The Third Reich believed strategic bombing would not be required in its conquest of Europe – and heavy bombers needed more raw materials to build; materials that were in short supply in pre-war Germany.

German fighters attended by Luftwaffe mechanics.

Messerschmitt Bf 109

The Messerschmitt Bf 109, often abbreviated to Me 109 or Bf 109, was the first truly modern fighter of the period and remained the backbone of the Luftwaffe's fighter force until late into World War II. It performed numerous roles, being used as an interceptor, bomber escort, fighter-bomber and ground attack aircraft. The Luftwaffe's three top Aces all flew the Bf 109, chalking up 928 victories between them. In total over 33,000 were produced, more than any other German aircraft of the war, and more than any other single fighter plane design in history.

A 1933 German military report identified the need for a single seat fighter, *Rüstungsflugzeug* III, which would be fast and mobile at all altitudes up to 32,000 ft (10,000m). The fighter would be powered by the Junkers Jumo 210 engine and armed with MG machine guns or cannons. When it became clear that the plane was developing more rapidly than the engine, designer Willi Messerschmitt turned to the British Rolls Royce Kestrel engine.

The first prototype of the new plane was completed in May 1935 and the Messerschmitt Bf 109 was unveiled to the public during the 1936 Berlin Olympics. The all-metal monoplane with retractable undercarriage and enclosed cockpit was a giant leap forward from the traditional wooden framed biplanes of earlier years, and it was clear that the Luftwaffe now had at its disposal the most modern fighter plane on the planet.

The Bf 109 was a potent weapon in the hands of an experienced pilot, and it was responsible for more aerial kills than any other aircraft of World War II. The fact that a plane designed in the mid-1930s continued to be used in active service by the Swiss, Finnish and Romanian air forces until the late 1950s demonstrates just how revolutionary Messerschmitt's original design really was.

THE FEW OF THE RAF

DATELINE ... 18 JUNE 1936 ... 1 SEPTEMBER 1939

On the northern side of the English Channel, Britain was taking a very different view of how the coming conflict would unfold. Everyone knew that, with a Nazi land invasion imminent, the future of the United Kingdom lay in the skies of World War II and rested in the hands of the RAF. There was, however, a major problem. The RAF was suffering from a severe absence of aircraft.

Building The Legends

After World War I, the RAF endured drastic government cuts, and the prelude to World War II saw it struggling to re-equip itself and train new pilots. 'Article XV squadrons' were formed from the air forces of British Commonwealth countries, and exiled pilots from occupied Europe were hastily added to the ranks of the RAF. Including the new foreign-born personnel, new British pilots freshly trained and former pilots retrained, the RAF numbered around 167,000 men in total. It was divided into Fighter Command, Bomber Command and Coastal Command. The job of Fighter Command was to defend the UK, while Bomber Command was charged with taking the offensive to the enemy and Coastal Command with defending shipping. All three would operate together to play a crucial role in the outcome of the war.

In terms of military hardware, the British were far behind the Luftwaffe, and were forced to rely on obsolete Fairey Battle bombers and Fairey Swordfish biplane fighters to supplement their meagre force of more modern and capable aircraft. In August 1939, the British had 2,573 planes, of which 1,313 were bombers and 773 fighters. Overseas aircraft in the Commonwealth swelled the figure to 3,250. However not all of the RAF's planes were fully operational and available for battle: Fighter Command had 373 operational aircraft at its disposal, Bomber Command 414 and Coastal Command 171, giving a total of just 958 aircraft. These included 167 Hawker Hurricanes and 104 Supermarine Spitfires, and the production of more of these fighters was the absolute priority throughout 1939.

British factories worked overtime day and night to turn out close to 500 fighter planes a month in advance of the expected German invasion. This was a rate Nazi Germany could not match, not least because German factories built so many different planes rather than specializing in production of a single aircraft. Messerschmitt, for example, built not only the Bf 109 fighter, but also a range of heavy fighters and fighter-bombers (the Bf 110, Me 210 and Me 410) along with gliders and reconnaissance aircraft. Whereas British factories concentrated on just two – the Supermarine Spitfire and the Hawker Hurricane – the two legendary aircraft that would rip apart the Luftwaffe in the skies over Britain.

Interception and Invasion

Britain had one other ace up its sleeve: radar. By the outbreak of the war, on-board radar was already being fitted to RAF planes, and two networks of radar stations had been constructed along the south coast of England throughout the 1930s. 'Chain Home' could detect formations of aircraft flying over the coast of France, enabling the RAF to scramble fighters to intercept them. 'Chain Home Low' detected low flying aircraft, which prevented any enemy surprise attacks.

Over 50 of these radar stations ensured that British defensive sorties could be co-ordinated swiftly and effectively. Their communication skills would soon be tested to their limits, as Adolf Hitler's frustration at Germany's slow progress boiled over and he sent the Panzers of the Third Reich rolling towards Poland. The Nazi invasion of Europe had begun.

RAF fighter pilots scrambling for their Spitfires.

THE INVASION OF POLAND

DATELINE ... 1 SEPTEMBER 1939 ... 6 OCTOBER 1939

The *Fall Weiss* (Case White) Operation, as the Germans code-named the invasion of Poland, was heavily dependent on the use of massive aerial power from the formidable German Air Force. Bombers destroyed 75% of the town of Wielun on the first day of the conflict, and Polish supply and communication lines were also decimated. The Poles had anticipated holding out against the Nazi invasion for at least three months; time enough for the promised help from her French and British allies to arrive. In the event, the country fell in little over a month.

The Day the War Began

Just after dawn on 1 September 1939, a German Stuka pilot spotted a Polish PZL P.11c in the skies above Krakow. He opened fire with his 7.92mm MG 17 machine guns, sending a hail of bullets straight through the fuselage of his fleeing opponent. German Flying Ace Frank Neubert then wheeled away into the clouds and returned to base, his mission a complete success. His opposite number, Captain Mieczyslaw Medwecki of the *Lotnictwo Wojskowe* (Polish Air Force), fought desperately to control his badly damaged plane as it hurtled towards the ground. But his situation was hopeless. He was about to become the first victim of the most savage air war the planet has ever seen. Medwecki was one of many to lose their lives cruelly on the day that World War II began.

The Power of the Luftwaffe

Contrary to popular belief, the Polish Air Force was not destroyed on the ground at the start of the war. Most of her aircraft had been dispersed to secret airfields ahead of the start of hostilities. Poland simply had too few aircraft, and the planes she did have were too slow to take on the modern air fleet that Germany had deployed in the battle. The PZL P.11 fighters could not catch the Luftwaffe's high-speed bombers, let alone take on the fighters on anything approaching an equal footing. Anti-aircraft guns were concentrated around Warsaw yet Poland initially elected to try and mount a defence of her borders, where the Luftwaffe bombers could target troop positions without being troubled by significant flak.

Polish bombers, by contrast, were sent on near-suicidal missions to attack the heavily

defended advancing German troop columns, resulting in catastrophic losses that depleted the air force's limited resources even further. As airfields were overrun or destroyed by bombing, Polish air units retreated inland. With supply lines cut, however, the Poles could not repair or resupply their aircraft, and they had to be abandoned or taken to the safety of Romania. Ground crews struggled to rendezvous at the few remaining operational airfields, and without them the remaining planes available could not be put into the sky.

On the ground, anti-aircraft guns ran out of ammunition, leaving Warsaw at the mercy of German bombers. On one day alone, 25 September 1939, over 1,000 sorties were flown by the Luftwaffe, and 550 tons of high explosives and incendiary bombs fell on the city. All other pockets of resistance endured similarly ruthless attacks. When the Soviet Red Army invaded from the East on 17 September, it had no need to fear the already shattered Polish Air Force, and its progress was swift. Although Poland never formally surrendered, the loss of the country was inevitable after the loss of her skies. The astonishing speed of the German victory shocked the entire world, and clearly demonstrated the vital role that air power would play in the unfolding world war.

The Unyielding Courage of Poland

The Polish Air Force had not gone down without a fight. They had inflicted heavy losses on the Luftwaffe, despite being outnumbered by almost five to one, and fighting with vastly inferior aircraft. The 300 almost obsolete Polish planes, and anti-aircraft fire, accounted for 126 enemy aircraft before Poland succumbed. Had Poland ever received the 14 RAF Hurricanes and 36 Fairey Battle planes that she had purchased from the Britain, even greater damage would undoubtedly have been inflicted upon the German invaders.

The ships carrying the vital planes from Liverpool were rerouted to Romania once hostilities commenced, however, and were effectively lost to the Polish Air Force when Romania broke its alliance with Poland and declared itself neutral. The planes were not significant to the overall outcome of the battle though. Far more telling was the lack of any concerted military assistance from France or Britain.

The Polish plan was based on the assumption that support would be forthcoming from her allies – but in the end assistance never arrived. Neither France nor the UK were adequately prepared for war against the mighty German military machine, and France's Saar Offensive, an invasion of Germany designed to draw German divisions and aircraft away from Poland, soon faded away. As Hitler and his generals had predicted, Poland was essentially left to defend herself alone.

When the last fighting unit of the Polish Army surrendered on 6 October, it must have seemed that all Polish resistance to the Third Reich was at an end. But significantly several thousand highly trained Polish airmen had escaped. They regrouped in exile beneath banners that declared *Love Demands Sacrifice* – soon adopted as the Polish Air Force's unofficial motto. Many of the pilots made their way into France and the United Kingdom. It was towards the skies of these countries that the Luftwaffe now turned its gaze, and there the vanquished yet unbowed Polish pilots would return to haunt their tormentors in the coming months and years.

(Left) German Messerschmitt Bf 109 being prepared for the invasion of Poland.

STANISLAW SKALSKI

The top Polish Ace of WWII, and the first Allied Ace of the war, was Stanislaw Skalski, credited with 18 confirmed kills and two probables. He shot down six German aircraft in the Battle of Poland before joining the RAF to assist in the Battle of Britain. The squadron he was assigned to, 501 Squadron, had a high percentage of Polish pilots who played a pivotal role in defending Britain, flying first Hawker Hurricanes and later Supermarine Spitfires. Fellow Pole Antoni Glowacki became the first ever Allied 'Ace' when he shot down five German aircraft in one day on 24 August 1940. Skalski himself was responsible for shooting down four planes during the battle, despite being hospitalized for six weeks after being shot down on 5 September 1940.

In October 1943 Skalski became commander of 'Skalski's Circus', otherwise known as the Polish Fighting Team, a Special Flight consisting of 15 experienced Polish pilots. The unit claimed a total of 26 kills during a two month period. Skalski was then assigned command of 601 Squadron, becoming the first Pole to command an RAF squadron.

After the war he joined the Air Force of the Polish Army, but was arrested by the communist regime in 1948 and sentenced to death after being found guilty of espionage. The sentence was later commuted to life imprisonment and Skalski was eventually released in 1956, rejoining the Polish Air Force and reaching the rank of *General brygady* (Brigadier General). He died in Warsaw on 12 November 2004, aged 88.

THE CALM BEFORE THE STORM

The Winter War in Finland (see p. 88) had illustrated the importance of tactics and training in aerial combat, and gave heart to those in the West facing the seemingly invincible forces of Nazi Germany. The lessons learned would help the Royal Air Force defend the British Isles in the summer of 1940. But before the Luftwaffe could deploy their full power against Britain, Nazi Germany had first to take France. Throughout 1939 the Allied and Axis forces were both preparing for the coming war, launching reconnaissance and exploratory raids to pinpoint each other's strengths and weaknesses.

The Sitzkrieg War

Within hours of the Anglo-French declaration of war on 3 September 1939, Royal Air Force Whitley bombers were thundering towards Germany, with orders to drop their payloads over key German towns and cities. They were not carrying high explosives, however. Instead, 13 tons of paper fluttered down over Germany. Six million leaflets warned Germans of the terrible consequences of the coming war, predicting that it would be long and bloody and would end in the defeat and destruction of their country.

These so-called 'Confetti Bombs' of propaganda leaflets were dropped by both sides in an attempt to persuade the civilian populations to rise up against their respective leaders and halt the slide to war. They failed in that objective, and many

pilots resented risking their lives in order to drop harmless 'Bullshit Bombs', but higher up the command chain it was decided that these 'dummy raids' were worthwhile and should continue.

The raids demonstrated that British bombers could reach deep into Germany, and even to Berlin, contrary to the proclamations of the Nazi leaders Hermann Göring and Joseph Goebbels. Each sortie triggered air-raid warnings that caused disquiet within the population and disrupted production at Germany factories. Not only did the leaflets themselves have to be collected and destroyed by German troops, but the information contained within them had to be countered by Nazi party officials. But perhaps most importantly, the pilots of the bombers were gaining priceless experience that would serve them well in future raids on 'real' German targets, when they would be dropping real bombs.

Dogfights and Evacuations

Horrific memories of World War I were still fresh in the minds of the European powers, and after Britain and France declared war on Germany on 3 September 1939, the expectation was that heavy fighting would begin soon afterwards. But 'total war' never came. Instead both sides settled into an uneasy lull in the fighting. Winston Churchill called it 'The Twilight War', while Americans called it 'The Phoney War'. The British press with typical cynicism called it *Sitzkrieg* (The Sitting War).

Pilots in the skies above France and Britain engaged in mock dogfights, as civilians were evacuated from the major towns and cities considered most vulnerable to attack. Barrage balloons were launched and blackouts imposed. Dummy aircraft and airfields were created to confuse attacking bombers. Fuel and ammunition was stored and factories turned out the raw materials of war by day and night.

Air Chief Marshal Sir Lewis Hodges, who would later receive several commendations for his role in the war, provided a vivid first-hand account of the reaction of RAF personnel on the ground to the news that war had been declared.

At the outbreak of war, on September 3rd 1939, I was in the hangars at Finningley with other members of the squadron listening to the broadcast by Neville Chamberlain that a state of war now existed between our country and the Germans. I remember this dramatic moment very clearly. We rushed out of the hangars on to the tarmac and looked out towards the east coast expecting to see German bombers coming over immediately.

Air Chief Marshal Sir Lewis Hodges
Speech at The Bomber Command Association

Battle of Barking Creek

Pilot Officer Montague Hulton-Harrop, was the first British airman killed in World War II, just three days after the war began. Ironically and tragically, his Hawker Hurricane was shot down by friendly fire. RAF Supermarine Spitfires mistook him for a German fighter. The debacle happened after an early morning air raid warning over Barking Creek, Essex, on the east coast of England, on 6 September 1939.

Number 56 Squadron stationed at RAF North Weald in Essex, was scrambled to intercept the enemy, and two Pilot Officers from the squadron were instructed to follow at a distance in a pair of reserve Hurricanes. Spitfires of 74 Squadron from RAF Hornchurch in Essex were also scrambled to deal with the supposed air raid. The two reserve Hurricanes from 56 Squadron were spotted by the 74 Squadron fighters who opened fire on them.

Few British pilots at this time had ever seen a German aircraft in flight and communication between aircraft and command stations was poor. Both of the Hurricanes were shot down, and Hulton-Harrop was killed instantly after being hit in the back of the head by machine-gun fire. The incident highlighted the inadequacy of RAF radar and identification procedures. Urgent orders were immediately issued leading to a significant improvement in performance before the Battle of Britain. Twenty days after the Barking Creek incident, a Dornier Do 18 became the first German aircraft brought down by the British.

Battle of the Heligoland Bight

Meanwhile British fighters and bombers were tasked with the mission to find and bomb the German fleet which was believed to be anchored at the port of Wilhelmshaven near the Heligoland Islands in the North Sea.

Heavily armed with machine guns at the front and the rear, the RAF believed that its Wellington bombers were unstoppable when flying at high speed and in close formation. It would be impossible for German fighters to attack the bombers from the side.

During December 1939, overconfident commanders sent their invincible Wellingtons on a series of daylight raids on Wilhelmshaven. But the raid on 18 December affected Bomber Command's strategy for the rest of the war. Coming under intense attack from Bf 109s and Bf 110s, ten Wellingtons were shot down, two more were forced to ditch before getting back to Britain and three more were destroyed in crash landings. Only two German fighters were shot down for the loss of 15 bombers out of a force of 22. German pilots had shown the Wellington to be clearly vulnerable to attack from the side, and with no self-sealing fuel tanks, they easily burst into flames.

The disastrous raid led to an immediate tactical change at Bomber Command. All Wellingtons were urgently modified. Self-sealing fuel tanks were added to prevent the spread of fire, and guns were added on each side of the aircraft. Bomber Command abandoned daylight bombing and switched to night-time operations only, radically affecting bombing accuracy.

(Above) Barrage balloons were flown as a deterrent to Nazi dive bombers.

HAWKER HURRICANE

The workhorse of the RAF was widely overshadowed by the Spitfire, but the Hurricane accounted for well over 50% of RAF victories during the Battle of Britain. More than 14,000 had been built by the end of 1944. Sydney Camm designed the plane with economy in mind, so that jigs and tools used to make the earlier Hawker Fury could be pressed into service when manufacturing the new plane. It took just 10,300 man hours to produce a Hurricane, as opposed to 15,200 for a Spitfire.

Though undoubtedly a vast improvement over the RAF's biplane fighters, the Hurricane was already outdated by the time it entered service in December 1937. Fabric-covered wings were soon replaced by metal-covered wings which were much more durable and allowed the plane to dive at greater speed.

The simplicity of the Hurricane's design was its chief asset, as it was easy to fly and easy to repair.

Though slower than either the Spitfire or Bf 109, the Hurricane could turn more tightly than either, and it provided a steady gun platform as well as being capable of withstanding a great deal of punishment from enemy fire. Later versions were equipped with more modern Rolls Royce engines which improved the top speed to 342 mph, and fuel tanks were fire-proofed to reduce (although by no means eliminate) the risk of the plane bursting into flames when hit. Sea Hurricanes came into service in mid-1941 and flew from Royal Navy aircraft carriers over the next three years.

Werner Mölders

In 1939, the French Air Force fought several minor battles with the Luftwaffe, one of the early incidents involved the legendary German Flying Ace and battle-hardened veteran from the Spanish Civil War, 26-year-old Werner Mölders. His first kill of World War II came in the skies over Contz-les-Bains in northern France, near the French-German-Luxemburg borders, when he shot down a French Curtiss P-36 fighter.

Many of his later World War II victories came during the Battle of Britain, when he accounted for 53 RAF planes. When the Luftwaffe failed to secure air superiority over Britain, however, he was transferred east to support Operation Barbarossa. On the very first day of the German invasion of Russia, he added four more victories to his total, and he went on a week later to pass Baron Manfred von Richthofen's World War I record of 80 victories. Once he had surpassed 100 victories in mid-July 1941, he was awarded the Knight's Cross with Oak Leaves, Swords and Diamonds, but was also immediately grounded, considered too valuable a propaganda asset to risk any further combat time in the air.

Mölders spent the next few months of the war as Inspector General of Fighters. He was summoned to attend the funeral of Ernst Udet, the WWI flying ace, who had committed suicide in November 1941, but the Heinkel He 111 Mölders was flying in as a passenger crashed in bad weather at Breslau (Wroclaw in western Poland). Mölders was killed and given a state funeral in Berlin on 28 November 1941, aged 28.

ADOLPH 'SAILOR' MALAN

South-African born Adolph Malan earned the nickname 'Sailor' due to his early career in the Merchant Marine. Having joined the RAF in 1935, his first military engagement of World War II was the unfortunate 'friendly-fire' incident at Barking Creek. After excelling in the skies over Dunkirk in 1940, Malan was awarded the DFC, and he went on to command 74 Squadron during the Battle of Britain. He drew up rules of air combat which were disseminated throughout RAF Fighter Command and included 'Wait until you see the whites of their eyes' and 'Get in quick, hit hard, get out!'

Malan's official tally at the end of the war was 27 confirmed victories with at least three other probable victories, two unconfirmed victories and a share in seven others. Many of his victories came in the most trying circumstances whilst outnumbered in the skies above Britain. The character of 'Squadron Leader Skipper' in the 1969 film *Battle Of Britain* was based upon him. Having survived the war, Malan died in 1963 of Parkinson's Disease, aged 53.

Wing Commander Adolph 'Sailor' Malan (fifth from left), with Air Chief Marshal Hugh Dowding, in bowler hat, and other RAF pilots, outside the Air Ministry in London.

THE EVACUATION OF DUNKIRK

DATELINE ... 26 MAY 1940 ... 4 JUNE 1940

Britain had elected a tough and uncompromising new leader. Destined to lead his country in momentous times, Winston Churchill was up for the fight. He replaced Neville Chamberlain as wartime Prime Minister. Churchill was ready to repel the Reich. He continually articulated his resolute contempt for Hitler and Nazi Germany with his unflinching and defiant rhetoric. Perhaps he understood the prospects of the war better than Hitler. In May 1940, he kept repeating that the British would fight on ...

of France, the marauding Panzer divisions were inexplicably ordered to a standstill rather than advance upon Dunkirk and the French coast. The decision infuriated the German army.

The left wing, consisting of armoured and motorized forces, which has no enemy before it, will thus be stopped dead in its tracks upon direct orders from the Führer. Finishing off the encircled enemy has to be left to the air force.

Generaloberst Franz Halder
Supreme High Command of the German Army
24 May 1940

The Miracle of Dunkirk

It was clear that the war in France was rapidly turning into a catastrophe for the French and British. At Dunkirk, encircled and cut off by the German Army, trapped with their backs to the sea as the Panzers advanced, the situation for the British Expeditionary Force was hopeless. They needed a miracle to survive.

Despite the perilous circumstances of the retreating troops, Churchill refused to countenance any capitulation or armistice negotiations. Instead, Operation Dynamo, a brave rearguard action was formulated and a massive cross-channel evacuation from Dunkirk to England was ordered. Hitler did not realize what the rescue of 250,000 British troops would do to the nation's morale.

Critically, however, at the same time as Churchill was planning to get the troops out

> ## " ... We shall fight on the beaches ... "
> Winston S. Churchill

Many historians highlight the failure to finish off the Allies at Dunkirk as a military miscalculation by Adolf Hitler. However, the Official War Diary of the German Army states that it was *Generalfeldmarschall* Gerd von Rundstedt who stopped the advance, with the German Führer merely ratifying the decision after the event. Whether history was rewritten or the emphasis changed to protect Hitler's reputation, we will never know, however the cessation of the advance appeared to be in complete contradiction to Hitler's own previous orders, issued by German Supreme Headquarters.

Directive 13, as the order was known, explicitly called for the total annihilation of all forces at Dunkirk with the Luftwaffe ordered to massacre the troops on the beaches from the air. The Directive did seem to advocate a final aerial bombardment of the beaches, so there was indeed room for interpretation by the Army. Whatever the reason, the 'Halt Order' given to the Panzers provided the British Expeditionary Forces a little respite, and allowed a few days for Churchill and his commanders to organize the miraculous evacuation of Dunkirk.

Operation Dynamo

As a target from the air, the harbour at Dunkirk was a sitting duck. The town and port were set ablaze and was almost completely destroyed by hundreds of German dive bombers descending upon the stricken Allied troops. There were no jetties or piers left anywhere along the 20 miles (32 km) of sandy beaches, which meant even small vessels had to lie offshore while troops waded out to them. The East Mole (sea wall) was used to land large ships but the retreating troops remained totally at the mercy of the Luftwaffe's bombing and strafing raids.

An urgent appeal from the Ministry of Shipping led to 700 private boats ('little ships') sailing the 39 nautical miles from Ramsgate, Kent and the small towns on the south coast of England into the furious cauldron of Dunkirk to ferry homewards the survivors and those that remained of the wounded and dying. In a speech to Parliament immediately after Operation Dynamo had been completed, Churchill described the terrifying German attack as outrageous slaughter.

Their main power, the power of their far more numerous air force, was thrown into the battle or else concentrated upon Dunkirk and the beaches ... They sent repeated waves of hostile aircraft, sometimes more than a hundred strong in one formation, to cast their bombs upon the single pier that remained and upon the sand dunes upon which the troops had their eyes for shelter.

British Prime Minister Winston S. Churchill
Westminster, London 1940

Dogfight over Dunkirk

The French coast was within range of southern England's Spitfire squadrons, and 16 of them took to the skies in an attempt to prevent the massacre of the Allied troops. The RAF flew a total of 3,561 sorties in nine days, 2,739 of them by fighters. They were almost always massively outnumbered by Luftwaffe fighters and fighter-bombers, and yet they continued to engage the vast enemy formations and hamper the Luftwaffe's attempts to reach Dunkirk. One RAF pilot, 23-year-old Robert Stanford Tuck, became an Ace in the first two days of Operation Dynamo, and was awarded the Distinguished Flying Cross (DFC) after downing three fighters and two bombers.

During May, 1940, this officer led his flight in company with his squadron on two offensive patrols over Northern France. As a result of one of these patrols in which the squadron engaged a formation of some 60 enemy aircraft, the Squadron Commander was later reported missing, and the flight commander wounded and in hospital. Flight Lieutenant Tuck assumed command, and on the following day led the squadron, consisting of only eight aircraft, on a further patrol engaging an enemy formation of fifty aircraft. During these engagements the squadron has shot down ten enemy aircraft and possibly another twenty-four. Throughout the combats this officer has displayed great dash and gallantry.

Flight Lieutenant Robert Roland Stanford Tuck
92 Squadron, RAF Croydon, Spitfire pilot
DFC Citation, 11 June 1940

Junkers Ju-87 Stuka

The two-man Junkers Ju-87 'Stuka' (from *Sturzkampfflugzeug*, the German for dive-bomber) first flew in combat in 1936 during the Spanish Civil War. Its infamous 'Jericho Trumpet' wailing siren was one of the most distinctive sounds of World War II, and heralded death and destruction for countless numbers of Allied servicemen — and civilians — between 1939 and 1945.

Around 6,500 of Hermann Pohlmann's aircraft were produced and the Stuka was still in use at the end of the war, due to no materially better design having been found. The very first aerial victory of the war, on 1 September 1939, was also scored by a Stuka. Throughout the Battle of Poland, the Stuka played a decisive role, on one occasion trapping six entire Polish divisions and forcing them to surrender after a relentless four-day attack.

The Battle of Britain, however, revealed just how vulnerable the Ju-87 was to attack from modern fighters. Slow, and with relatively modest weaponry, the Stuka was only really suited to conditions where Bf 109s and Fw 190s had already established air superiority. It was withdrawn from the Battle of Britain after catastrophic losses were sustained throughout July and August 1940. Though Stukas would later claim the lives of many thousands of Soviet ground troops in the battle for Eastern Europe, in the West its role was more minor as increasingly large numbers of RAF Spitfires and USAAF P-51 Mustangs prowled the skies.

ROBERT STANFORD TUCK

Born in 1916, Robert Stanford Tuck joined the RAF in 1935, he became a Squadron Leader then Wing Commander. He was awarded a second DFC during the Battle of Britain in October 1940 and a DSO (Distinguished Service Order) in January 1941. He was eventually shot down over the English Channel and became a prisoner of war. He died at home in Canterbury, Kent in 1987, aged 70.

Feeling Abandoned

The Luftwaffe lost 132 aircraft during Operation Dynamo, and the RAF lost 99. Despite the RAF's heroic efforts, many of the troops on the beaches felt forgotten by the RAF. The British fighters usually engaged the Luftwaffe far from the beaches and when battle did take place near the troops, low cloud often hid the dogfights. If the skies were clear, the RAF fighters were more than likely to be shot at by their own side.

As the mists and clouds dispersed, many aircraft appeared on the scene and fighters constantly came low over us. More often than not they were Spitfires, but our ships were not taking chances and nearly always opened fire indiscriminately on them. As this kept happening, I hoisted 6-flag – cease fire – and blew the siren to draw attention and try and stop the firing. In spite of this I can remember our own machine-gun aft in Keith firing away regardless of the 'cease fire' gong. Once they started firing, they could hear nothing.

Rear Admiral Wake-Walker, HM Keith, Royal Navy
Dunkirk Evacuation, May 1940

New Zealander Alan Deere, an RAF Ace who was shot down over Northern France and making his way back home with the evacuated troops, expressed his frustration at the troops' ingratitude.

For two weeks non-stop I had flown my guts out, and this was all the thanks I got. What was the use of trying to explain that the RAF had patrolled further inland, often above cloud, with the insuperable task of covering adequately a patrol line from Ostend to Boulogne?

Flying Officer Alan Deere, 54 Squadron
RAF Hornchurch, Spitfire pilot, aged 23

More than a Turning Point

Originally, it was thought that some 45,000 soldiers might be rescued. Eventually, 338,226 were taken away in what Churchill described as a 'miracle of deliverance'. It was undoubtedly a key turning point in the war, and without the bravery and determination of Royal Air Force pilots far more of the 700 or so 'little ships' that thronged Dunkirk to evacuate the troops would have been destroyed.

It did not matter how strong we were, they went for us as if we were sheep and they fought us at any odds. Our orders were to reach Dunkirk and bomb the British Army and Navy out of existence, but your mad pilots turned the skies into a mad house.

Anonymous captured German pilot, shot down over Northern France

Victory from the Jaws of Defeat

Although the troops on the ground were disgruntled, the view from the safe haven of Central Operation Rooms in Uxbridge on the outskirts of London was different. The Air Officer Commanding No. 11 Group, which was largely responsible for taking on the Luftwaffe, was Air Vice-Marshal Keith Park. His formal report after Operation Dynamo made clear his pride at what the RAF had achieved.

Our fighter pilots obtained such ascendency over the German bombers that during the last phase of the operation the German bombers jettisoned their bombs in the sea on sighting even small formations of our fighters. On one occasion, a fighter pilot who had used up all his ammunition made a feint attack at a sub-formation of German bombers who immediately fled east, one of them losing control and crashing in the sea.

*Air Vice-Marshal Keith Park
Group 11 Operations Commander, RAF Uxbridge*

" ... We shall never surrender ..."
Winston S. Churchill

A certain disaster had been turned into a celebrated victory. Hitler did not understand the British well enough. During Dunkirk he remarked that the sight of a beaten army often breaks the spirit of an entire nation. But he could not see the lines of cheering people waving at the smiling soldiers leaning out of the train windows on their way home from Dunkirk and Dover. The British did not regard the returning soldiers as those of a beaten army. A defiant Winston Churchill declared the success of the evacuation to the House of Commons on 4 June 1940. His words ring down through the ages, epitomizing the determined Dunkirk spirit with which Britain became associated in the darkest days of World War II.

We shall go on to the end. We shall fight in France, we shall fight on the seas and oceans, we shall fight with growing confidence and growing strength in the air, we shall defend our Island, whatever the cost may be. We shall fight on the beaches, we shall fight on the landing grounds, we shall fight in the fields and in the streets, we shall fight in the hills; we shall never surrender.

*British Prime Minister Winston S. Churchill
Westminster, London, 4 June 1940*

Well, another day is gone, and with it a whole lot of grand blokes. Got another brace of 109s today, but the whole Luftwaffe seems to leap on us – we were hopelessly outnumbered. I was caught napping by a 109 in the middle of a dogfight, and got a couple of holes in the aircraft, one of them filled the office with smoke, but the Jerry overshot and he's dead. If anyone says anything to you in the future about the inefficiency of the RAF – I believed the BEF troops were booing the RAF in Dover the other day – tell them from me we only wish we could do more. But without aircraft we can do no more than we have done – that is, our best, and that's fifty times better than the German best, though they are fighting under the most advantageous conditions. I know

of no RAF pilot who has refused combat yet – and that sometimes means combat with odds of more than fifty to one. Three of us the other day had been having a fight, and were practically out of ammunition and juice when we saw more than eighty 109s with twelve Ju 87s, all the same we gave them combat, so much so that they left us alone in the end – on their side of the Channel too. This is not a tale of stirring heroism. It is just the work that we all do. One of my sergeants shot down three fighters and a bomber before they got him – and then he got back in a paddle steamer. So don't worry, we are going to win this war even if we have only one aeroplane and one pilot left – the Boche could produce the whole Luftwaffe and you would see the one pilot and the one aeroplane go into combat. All that sounds very involved, but I am trying to convey to you something of the spirit of Per ardua ad astra today. The spirit of the average pilot has to be seen to be believed.

Flight Lieutenant R.D.G. Wright, Squadron 213, Hurricane pilot. Letter home 31 May 1940

(This incredible insight into the effort put in by the RAF during Operation Dynamo was provided by a British pilot writing home to his mother on 31 May 1940. It is doubtful if Wright ever did get home again to see his mother as he was killed ten weeks later during the Battle of Britain.)

(Above) Evacuation of troops from Dunkirk.

THE BATTLE OF BRITAIN

At 05:15 hours on 10 July 1940, five high explosive bombs fell on Martlesham Heath Aerodrome in the south of England. The all-out German aerial assault, designed to pave the way for an invasion of Britain, had begun. There were many scores to settle. Nations such as Norway, Denmark, Holland, Luxemburg, Poland, Austria, Czechoslovakia, Belgium and France all pinned their hopes on an RAF victory in the skies over Britain.

The Battle of Britain

France had formally surrendered to Germany on 25 June 1940 and with the Battle of France now won, the Luftwaffe embarked upon the Battle of Britain. It would be the first major campaign fought entirely in the air. Of the 3,000 pilots who flew in the Battle of Britain, roughly 20 per cent came from overseas, not only from the British Commonwealth but also from the occupied nations of Europe, many with a grudge against the Nazis.

What General Weygand has called the Battle of France is over. I expect that the Battle of Britain is about to begin. Upon this battle depends the survival of Christian civilization. Upon it depends our own British life, and the long continuity of our institutions and our Empire. The whole fury and might of the enemy must very soon be turned on us. Hitler knows that he will have to break us in this island or lose the war. If we can stand up to him, all Europe may be freed and the life of the world may move forward into broad, sunlit uplands. But if we fail, then the whole world,

including the United States, including all that we have known and cared for, will sink into the abyss of a new dark age made more sinister, and perhaps more protracted, by the lights of perverted science. Let us therefore brace ourselves to our duties, and so bear ourselves, that if the British Empire and its Commonwealth last for a thousand years, men will still say, 'This was their finest hour'.

British Prime Minister Winston S. Churchill
Westminster, London, 18 June 1940

Selling My Soul to the Devil

In the first weeks of the war, the Luftwaffe targeted airfields and shipping convoys in the English Channel in what came to be described as the *Kanalkampf* (or Channel battle) phase of the operation. Mines were also dropped in the Channel. The losses inflicted upon shipping eventually led to the British Admiralty aborting all convoys through the Channel – but the RAF had also managed to down large numbers of Luftwaffe bombers and fighters. Crucially, the impact on Fighter Command was minimal – only 74 pilots were lost.

In addition, RAF Spitfire and Hurricane pilots were gaining valuable combat experience – the average age of pilots was just 20 years old, and unlike their counterparts in the Luftwaffe many had yet to become battle-hardened.

It fascinates me beyond belief to see my bullets striking home and then to see the Hun blowing

Geoffrey Page went on to become a Wing Commander and British Flying Ace with 17 kills. He claimed the first three of his kills in the middle weeks of July 1940, when he was only 20 years old. He was shot down during the Battle of Britain, but died peacefully in the year 2000, aged 80.

up before me. It also makes me feel sick. Where are we going and how will it all end? I feel as if I'm selling my soul to the devil. I need someone to talk to who isn't tied up in this legalized murder.

Pilot Officer Geoffrey Page,
56 Squadron, RAF Hurricane pilot

Eagle Day

Poor weather over England then prevented full scale Luftwaffe raids until the middle of August, and this relative lull in fighting was used to give the Luftwaffe time to recover from its losses in the Battle of France and prepare for a more sustained attack.

The main campaign – Göring's Operation *Adlerangriff* (Eagle Attack) – began on 12 August 1940, with the decisive *Adlertag* (Eagle Day) hammer blow set to be delivered on 13 August. On 12 August, the Luftwaffe tried to blind the British by targeting radar stations. The station at Ventnor on the Isle of Wight was badly damaged and several others were lightly damaged, but all were fully operational again by the morning of 13 August. Britain awoke to another day of poor weather, and so no major attack from Germany was expected. Göring had, in fact, officially postponed Eagle Day, but the message did not reach many of his crews in time, and so they set off on their missions as previously planned.

Tracked by British radar from the moment they entered formation in the Amiens area of northern France, the German bombers were intercepted by squadrons of Spitfires and Hurricanes. At around 06:30 hours, the first combats of the day began. Five German Dornier Do 17s were destroyed and a further seven badly damaged. Two Hurricanes were lost on the RAF side. In heavy fighting throughout the rest of the day, the skies above Britain filled with German and British aircraft.

The main targets for the Luftwaffe were aerodromes, shipping and industry.

Southampton docks, on the south coast of England, the Nuffield Aeroplane Factory in Birmingham and Detling Aerodrome in Kent, south-east England, were among those suffering the most damage. According to RAF combat reports, they shot down a total of 78 German bombers and fighter escorts, and chalked up a further 33 'probables' and 49 'damaged'. Given the scale of the raids, RAF losses were slight – eleven Hurricanes and two Spitfires.

Since early on the 13th August, enemy aircraft activity over this country has been on a scale far in excess of anything hitherto carried out … All these raids were intercepted by our fighters which suffered very few losses but inflicted heavy casualties on the enemy.

Summary of Adlertag by RAF Fighter Command

As night fell on Göring's Eagle Day, the German attacks faded. *Adlertag* was over, and it had been a major defeat for the Luftwaffe. But Göring and Hitler, were unflinching in their determination to break the British. In the coming weeks even greater numbers of German fighters and bombers were thrown into the battle, culminating on 18 August 1940 with the largest attack of all, when 2,200 aircrew were sent across the English Channel. The RAF would later remember it as 'The Hardest Day'.

The targets were RAF airfields; the size of the attacking forces vast. Throughout the previous week the Luftwaffe had remorselessly hammered away at the RAF, sending wave after wave of bombers to attack key infrastructure targets. Bf 109s provided fighter cover and the sheer number of aircraft involved meant that Britain's pilots were close to exhaustion, and the RAF itself close to collapse.

Island of Last Hope

At around midday on 18 August, the first of three giant Luftwaffe formations crossed the English Channel. Dornier Do 17, Junkers Ju 88 and Heinkel He 111 bombers were escorted by Bf 109 and Bf 110 fighters. Southern English airfields were the primary target. A second wave of Stukas, supported by Bf 109s, would press home the attack before a third giant wave of mixed bombers and fighters sought to finish the job. Against such a force, British anti-aircraft guns were wholly inadequate. Biggin Hill airfield in Kent was in part defended by World War I vintage 3 inch guns and at RAF Kenley they resorted to firing cables attached to parachutes in the hope they would snag attacking bombers' wings. Renamed by Polish pilots in exile as 'The Island of Last Hope', Britain's 'last hope' was its Spitfires and Hurricanes.

Both sides lost more aircraft on this day than on any other during the Battle of Britain. German intelligence suggested that RAF Fighter Command had been so mauled by previous encounters with the Luftwaffe that it was now down to just 300 operational aircraft. A combination of exaggerated claims of kills by German pilots and an underestimation of British production capacity meant that the figure was wildly inaccurate: the RAF had some 1,400 fighters remaining, more than in July 1940.

A Devious Strategy

The plan devised by Luftwaffe Commanders Albert Kesselring and Hermann Göring was to concentrate all of the Luftwaffe's fire-power on a relatively modest list of targets in the hope of weakening Fighter Command's capacity to put planes into the air. To this end, RAF Kenley in Surrey, RAF North Weald in Essex, RAF Hornchurch in Essex and RAF Biggin Hill in Kent were selected as the primary targets.

RAF Kenley was first to be attacked, by a Staffel (small flying unit) of nine Do 17 bombers. They came in at tree top level taking the airfield out of commission for two hours, destroying eight Hurricanes on the ground. However, a delayed attack by a much larger force of Do 17s and Ju 88s with a mission to destroy Kenley's anti-aircraft guns meant the Staffel was surprised by an unexpectedly courageous counter-attack by the airfield's gunners. Four of the nine Do 17s were shot down, two more were seriously damaged and three were slightly damaged.

Meanwhile, heavy bomber formations were attempting to strike at RAF Biggin Hill. The main formation of Ju 88 and Do 17s was scattered by three squadrons of Spitfires and Hurricanes, however, and as a consequence the majority missed their targets. The Heinkel He 111s of KG 1 fared better. Their Bf 109 escort fighters had managed to defend them on the journey, engaging the RAF fighters so that the bombers had a clear run at their target.

They failed to inflict serious damage on the airfield, however, and the personnel at Biggin Hill had time to take cover, meaning casualties were slight. As the German formations withdrew, the RAF jumped on them, and the Luftwaffe's Messerschmitt Bf 109s could do little to prevent the waves of Spitfires and Hurricanes from picking off many of the bombers. The Bf 110 escorts were incapable of matching the RAF fighters, and after suffering catastrophic losses were soon withdrawn from the battle altogether.

Enduring Heavy Losses

Of the four Ju 87 Stuka groups sent to attack the Sussex bases RAF Poling and RAF Ford, three managed to find their targets and cause considerable damage. Ten Stuka dive bombers of StG 77, were destroyed by Hurricanes of 43 and 601 Squadrons, along with six Bf 109s escorts. By the end of this wave of German attacks, only RAF Ford in Sussex and RAF Gosport in Hampshire had suffered significant damage and crucially British radar remained operational.

By contrast the Luftwaffe had sustained serious losses, but the battered air force was soon back in action for a final massive attack launched by 250 aircraft at around 17:00 hours. Low cloud prevented the 51 He 111s of KG 53 from hitting their intended target of RAF North Weald in Essex, and most ended up dumping their payloads in the sea. Four bombers were shot down and 13 of their escorting Bf 110s were either destroyed or damaged. The 58 Dornier 17s of KG 2 also struggled to drop their bombs with any accuracy on RAF Hornchurch in Essex and vicious dogfights between their Bf 109 escort fighters and RAF Hurricanes led to heavy losses for both sides.

Squandering the Advantage

The Luftwaffe and RAF each flew in excess of 900 sorties on The Hardest Day. Each side lost around 70 aircraft, though each at the time claimed to have destroyed many more. The Luftwaffe, however, lost many more pilots than the RAF. Five Germans were killed, wounded or taken prisoner, for every British airman lost. While neither side could afford to sustain the sort of massive losses suffered on The Hardest Day for long, the battle was an undoubted victory for the

RAF. The Luftwaffe had failed to demoralize Fighter Command and Hitler soon began to realize that his air force would be fatally weakened for future battles if he continued an aerial war of attrition.

Operation Sea Lion, the planned invasion of Britain, was now in serious jeopardy. In a desperate last attempt to deliver a decisive blow to the RAF, Hitler decided to launch a massive two-pronged attack on London. Having failed to destroy Fighter Command on the ground, the aim was now to annihilate it in the air. Hundreds of German aircraft, in two giant waves, gathered over the English Channel and, in formations up to 30 miles (48 km) wide, headed straight for the British capital.

In the preceding days, Germany had switched her attack from RAF Fighter Command's airfields to targets in and around London. Luftwaffe bombers had scored many successes and losses had been acceptable, so the assumption was that Fighter Command had been badly weakened and would be unable to defend the capital against a massive onslaught. The truth was that Fighter Command had indeed been depleted, but the cessation of attacks on its infrastructure had given it a vital breathing space. Switching away from the bombing of RAF airfields would prove to be a disastrous mistake.

Our greatest mistake was not keeping the pressure up on the airfields of southern England. Göring thought that by trying to bomb London by night he could devastate London and the people of Britain … This was his greatest mistake. He himself gave the RAF room to breathe, time to reorganize, time to rebuild. The result was, we were losing the Battle of Britain.

Generalleutnant Adolf Galland
Luftwaffe Flying Ace, 1940

Towering Citadel of London

By 15 September 1940, Air Vice-Marshal Keith Park's No. 11 Group based at RAF Uxbridge in the western outskirts of London was ready and able to take on the Luftwaffe, and Douglas Bader's 'Big Wing' at RAF Duxford in Cambridgeshire was also within striking distance of London. Göring's airmen, who took to the skies in the confident belief that the RAF were down to their last few dozen Spitfires, were in for a rude awakening.

By pure coincidence, British Prime Minister Winston Churchill was visiting No. 11 Group Operations Room on the morning that the German attack took place. He was therefore able to observe Commander Keith Park moving his defensive squadrons into place as the Luftwaffe formations were tracked by radar moving across the skies over the south-eastern county of Kent towards the capital. Just before noon, Hurricanes and Spitfires dived towards the enemy aircraft and battle was joined.

Swarms of Bf 109s defended the bombers and fierce dogfights raged as they sought to protect the slow and heavy Dorniers, Heinkels and Junkers from the wrath of the RAF. Although each side lost large numbers of planes, for the most part the Luftwaffe fighters managed to keep the bombers' path to London clear. However, the Bf 109s had used most of their fuel in the process.

By the time the citizens of London saw the bomber force approaching the outskirts of the city, the protecting German fighters had little or no fuel left and were forced to turn back. Just as the fighters were turning for home, Douglas Bader's Big Wing of 60 RAF fighters arrived from Duxford. Almost at once they were joined by Hurricanes and

Spitfires from squadrons that Air Vice-Marshal Park had until then held in reserve.

The massive fighter force flew full throttle at the virtually unprotected Luftwaffe bomber formations, causing panic amongst its airmen. One Do 17 front gunner later recalled that, 'it seemed that the whole of the RAF was there'. The Luftwaffe airmen had been assured that the RAF was 'close to extinction', and so the raiders assumed that every aircraft in England had been moved south to defend the capital. The sky was so full of British fighters that bombers were attacked by several different planes at once, each coming from a different direction.

Chaos in the Skies

The lumbering German bombers were forced to bank and dive in all directions to avoid the hail of bullets now raining in on them from the RAF fighters causing chaos, smoke and flames all over the skies above London. Many bombs were dropped at random, lightening the load to assist the bomber's swift escape from the battle zone. Residential and commercial areas of south London were badly affected, but the more important strategic targets the Luftwaffe was hoping to destroy were protected.

The retreating aircraft were chased as they withdrew and, without adequate fighter protection, many were destroyed before they could escape back across the Channel. So scattered were the Luftwaffe formations that the combat zone stretched to 85 miles (140 km) long and 38 miles (62 km) wide. By 12:30 hours, the British radar screens showed that the Germans were in full retreat, and the RAF pilots returned to their bases. Many must have thought that they had defeated the main German attack. The reality was

their day had only just begun. A second, even larger attack was already heading for London.

The Big Wing

The Germans hoped that the sheer weight of numbers would cripple the RAF this time. The Hurricanes and Spitfires that Air Vice-Marshal Park scrambled to defend London were greatly outnumbered by the attacking Luftwaffe force. Some estimates put the invading formation at over 600 planes. Radar, again, alerted the British to the seriousness of the threat, and by 14:35 hours every available aircraft had been committed to the battle. Winston Churchill asked Keith Park what reserves were available. The answer was none.

RAF Fighter Command's 276 Spitfires and Hurricanes were all that stood between Britain and defeat. Once more, the British pilots surged into the heart of the giant German formations and sent them scattering in panic. The German bombers that did manage to escape through the hail of gunfire were then greeted with the frightening sight of The Big Wing as they made their final approach to London.

Every squadron in 11 Group had intercepted, and at that moment I saw Douglas Bader's wing of five squadrons coming in from Duxford. This was the day that Göring had said to his fighters the RAF was down to their last 50 Spitfires. But they'd run up against twenty-three squadrons for a start, when they were on their way in, and then, when they got over London, with the Messerschmitt 109s running out of fuel, in comes Douglas Bader with sixty more fighters.

Flight Lieutenant Bobby Oxspring, 66 Squadron
20-year-old RAF Spitfire pilot, 1940

Fighting for their Lives

Brutal dogfights raged over the skies of southern England, as Bf 109s attempted to intervene between the RAF fighters and their prey. Some of the fiercest fighting was above London itself, as the RAF fought a desperate last-ditch battle to prevent the destruction of some of Britain's most famous landmarks. Fighting for their young lives, the Spitfire and Hurricane pilots displayed a remarkably relaxed coolness ... and some even had time for a bit of sight-seeing in the war-torn skies.

Our first attack broke them up pretty nicely. The Dornier I attacked with a burst lasting several seconds began to turn to the left away from his friends. I gave him five seconds, and he went away with white smoke streaming behind him. As I broke away and started to make a steep climbing turn, I looked over the side. I recognized the river [Thames] immediately below me through a hole in the clouds. I saw the bends and the bridges and idly wondered where I was. Then I saw Kennington Oval, and I thought to myself, 'That is where they play cricket'.

Squadron Leader John Sample, 501 Squadron
RAF Hurricane pilot, over Central London 1940

Resilient Defiance

The tough line of fearless RAF fighters held their positions obstinately, resolutely protecting their precious capital city. The German bombers were forced to veer off target and turn for home without dropping their bombs on their intended targets. They were ruthlessly pursued, and further serious losses were inflicted on the beleaguered Luftwaffe. In total, 56 German aircraft were shot down for the loss of 27 RAF fighters. What would afterwards be known as Battle

of Britain Day was a decisive turning point in the war. The Nazi invasion of Britain, scheduled to begin just two days later, was postponed indefinitely.

At one time you could see planes going down on fire all over the place, and the sky seemed full of parachutes. It was sudden death that morning, for our fighters shot them to blazes.

Squadron Leader Douglas Bader
The Big Wing Commander, RAF Duxford

Robert 'Bobby' Oxspring

Born in 1919, Bobby Oxspring was 20 years old when war broke out. Seen below in front of his Spitfire, Bobby went on to become one of the RAF's great Aces. He flew Spitfires throughout the Battle of Britain and fought in the North African campaign. He was promoted to Squadron Leader in 1944 and during the war claimed 13 solo kills with two shared. He died in 1989, aged 70.

Adolf Galland

Adolf 'Dolfo' Galland entered World War II with a wealth of combat experience from the Spanish Civil War, during which he flew over 300 missions and rose to the rank of Squadron Leader. Though his role in Spain was primarily concerned with ground attack and he used those same skills once again during the invasion of Poland, Galland persuaded his superiors to allow him to become a fighter pilot and tested his new skills flying Bf 109s in the Battle of France. He was fully prepared for the dogfights of the Battle of Britain in 1940, and rapidly became the scourge of the RAF, chalking up 40 confirmed kills by September of that year and receiving the Knight's Cross with Oak Leaves as a result.

In August 1941, Galland met the captured British legend Douglas Bader and showed him the cockpit of a Bf 109. The chivalrous Galland forwarded Bader's request for replacement artificial legs to be sent to him, along with a recommendation that the request be granted. He did, however, draw the line at allowing Bader's other request — that he be allowed to take the Messerschmitt for a spin.

By November 1940, Galland had passed 50 victories and risen to the rank of Colonel. Subsequent sorties over the English Channel saw Galland's tally of confirmed kills rise to 96 by November 1941, at which point he took over from Werner Mölders as *General der Jagdflieger* (Inspector of Fighters) after Mölders was killed in a flying accident. His role then changed from flying combat missions to commanding Luftwaffe forces in the increasingly savage aerial war over Europe. He clashed violently with Hermann Göring over how best to defend Germany from Allied bombing attacks, and their strained relationship broke down entirely in January 1945 when Galland was relieved of his command and placed under house arrest.

Galland was to make one last return to combat flying later the same year, when he was granted permission to form a jet fighter unit as Germany desperately sought to avoid defeat. The new unit, *Jagdverband 44*, caused a huge impact and downed many Allied planes, but its formation ultimately came too late to save the Luftwaffe which by then had been broken by incessant Allied attacks.

Galland finished the war with a total of 104 confirmed kills. He survived being shot down four times and after the war was employed by the Argentine government to organize its air force. He then returned to Germany in order to manage his own business. He died in 1996, aged 82.

Adolf Hitler (left) in conversation with Adolf Galland.

MAVERICK GENIUS

DOUGLAS BADER

Bader's courage and determination in the face of serious disability made him a legend in his own lifetime. Born in 1910 in St John's Wood, London, it was while staying with his uncle, who was then a Flight Lieutenant in the RAF, that Bader's interest in becoming a pilot was first awakened. His early career was marked with tragedy after he crashed a Bristol Bulldog in 1931 while showing off his aerobatic skills. The incident led to both his legs being amputated, one just above and one just below the knee.

When war was declared in September 1939, Bader reapplied to the RAF in the hope of seeing active service. With the country desperately short of trained pilots, he was accepted and posted with No. 19 Squadron at Duxford, Cambridgeshire. Two months later he was appointed Flight Commander of 222 Squadron, and by June 1940 he was commanding 242 Squadron.

Bader became obsessed with the concept of the 'Big Wing'; sending large numbers of fighter squadrons to simultaneously attack the invading Luftwaffe aircraft in the hope of dealing them a decisive blow. Together with Air Chief Marshal Trafford Leigh-Mallory, he put the plan into action. Initial successes were modest, but the tactic paid off handsomely when massive Luftwaffe attacks on London in September 1940 were repelled by the swarms of Hurricanes and Spitfires. Bader was awarded the Distinguished Flying Cross (DFC) for his contribution, and the Duxford Big Wing was credited with destroying 152 German aircraft.

Bader also copied the German *Schwarm* formation, called the 'finger-four' in England, which later became the standard formation for all modern air forces. His iconoclastic approach won him admirers and enemies in equal measure, but no one doubted his maverick genius. After engaging with enemy forces he would often unclip his oxygen mask in order to light up his pipe on the way home, and on the side of his plane was emblazoned the image of Hitler being kicked in the backside.

His fame spread to both sides of the English Channel. When Bader was captured by the Germans after he bailed out over Nazi-occupied France in August 1941 following a mid-air collision with a Messerschmitt Bf 109, the great and good of the Nazi party flocked to meet him. The Germans even agreed to allow a new false leg to be air-dropped to Bader, so keen were they to please their illustrious captive. Bader was finally released from Colditz Castle in the spring of 1945. Despite having been a prisoner for most of the war, his personal tally stood at 22.5 German aircraft. When he died of a heart attack at the age of 72, the *London Times* obituary described him as, 'The personification of RAF heroism during the Second World War.'

German Heinkel He III bomber over
the river Thames, London, 1940.

THE BLITZ

DATELINE ... 7 SEPTEMBER 1940 ... 21 MAY 1941

Adolf Hitler had finally begun to realize that Britain could not be conquered while the RAF remained such a formidable force. New tactics and a fresh strategy were required. If the British could not be defeated through the destruction of their Air Force, then the Nazis planned to beat them into submission through the remorseless bombing of their major cities at night.

Random Terror Attacks

Perhaps it was inevitable that 'total war' would lead to indiscriminate bombing of civilian targets. But both sides, at the start of the war, had maintained that they were strictly opposed to such a policy, and each later blamed the other for abandoning their commitment to stick to strictly military targets.

From the British perspective, the Germans had shown in the past their willingness to inflict widespread civilian casualties. The notorious attack on the Basque town of Guernica in northern Spain during the Spanish Civil War in 1937 led to hundreds of innocent lives being lost. Wielun, in Poland, was bombed in 1939 despite having no military targets of any real significance.

Germany claimed Polish troops were in the area, but Poland maintained it was simply a terror attack which killed 1,300 civilians, and pointed to the fact that Warsaw was also bombed indiscriminately some three weeks later. In 1939, Rotterdam in The Netherlands was also heavily bombed, despite surrender negotiations taking place at the time.

Germany claimed that the first terror attack against her civilians came when the British attacked the city of Freiburg im Breisgau in south-west Germany close to the French border on the edge of the Black Forest. On 10 May 1940, 22 children, 13 women and 11 male civilians were killed in an aircraft raid. A famous university town, Freiburg had no strategic significance and the attack provoked outrage in Germany. Many consider this incident as the moment Germany decided to attack British cities in retaliation.

Minor attacks, such as British bombs on Esbjerg and Western Germany, were ignored and not followed up by Luftwaffe reprisals. It was only in the weeks of crisis caused by the German offensive in the West, that the RAF began dropping bombs indiscriminately on German cities. The starting point was a raid on Freiburg im Breisgau and Heidelberg.

The military value of these raids, which were carried out on an utterly inadequate scale, was precisely nil. From a historical point of view they can only be regarded as acts of desperation. But the effect on Hitler and public opinion in Germany was certainly enormous. The German reply was not long in coming. The battle with England was now joined on the basis of unrestricted air war.

Oberst Werner Baumbach
Commander of Kampfgeschwader
(German secret bomber wing)

No one realized at the time, but when details later emerged it was apparent that the raid on

Freiburg im Breisgau was not an RAF attack at all, but a bungled Luftwaffe mission. Three German bombers became disoriented in bad weather and in their geographic confusion dropped their bombs, mistaking Freiburg for their official target, the French city of Dijon. Their elementary navigational error carried catastrophic consequences over the coming years for hundreds of thousands of civilians across Europe.

Mr Churchill has repeated the declaration that he wants war. About six weeks ago now, he launched this war in an arena in which he apparently believes he is quite strong: namely, in the air war against the civilian population, albeit beneath the deceptive slogan of a so-called war against military objectives. Ever since Freiburg, these objectives have turned out to be open cities, markets, villages, residential housing, hospitals, schools, kindergartens, and whatever else happens to be hit.

Up to now I have given little by way of response. This is not intended to signal, however, that this is the only response possible or that it shall remain this way. I am fully aware that with our response, which one day will come, will also come the nameless suffering and misfortune of many men. Naturally, this does not apply to Mr Churchill himself since by then he will surely be secure in Canada, where the money and the children of the most distinguished of war profiteers have already been brought.

But there will be great tragedy for millions of other men. And Mr Churchill should make an exception and place trust in me when as a prophet I now proclaim: A great world empire will be destroyed. A world empire which I never had the ambition to destroy or as much

as harm. Alas, I am fully aware that the continuation of this war will end only in the complete shattering of one of the two warring parties. Mr Churchill may believe this to be Germany. I know it to be England.

Führer Adolf Hitler, German Third Reich
19 July 1940

Unlimited Civilian Bombing

Another key moment in the prelude to the Blitz came on 24 August 1940, when German bombers veered off-course and dropped their payload over residential areas of London. The RAF bombed Berlin the next day, and although ostensibly targeting the Siemens factories and Tempelhof airfield they hit civilian targets. The military damage caused by the raid was negligible, but its perfect timing had a huge psychological impact on German Supreme Command as the bombing completely undermined a report by Göring to Hitler proclaiming the RAF had been smashed.

An outraged Adolf Hitler, incensed by both the Berlin bombing and Göring's exaggerated RAF report, sent direct orders that central London was to be bombed without delay in retaliation. From this point onwards, both sides launched concerted full-scale attacks on the main cities of their enemy. The Luftwaffe, lacking the heavy bombers required for a sustained strategic bombing campaign, relied on large numbers of medium bombers massing together over a single target.

Having failed to amass air superiority, the missions were highly dangerous and the Germans could not afford to lose precious pilots. In order to ensure that every bomb that fell counted, therefore, they developed a guidance system which was designed to lead the vast formations to a precise location and allow them to drop their bombs with great accuracy. The British, discovered the

Two of London's famous landmarks, the Tower of London (left) and Tower Bridge (right) after a German air raid on London docks, 1940.

German system and immediately set about trying to disrupt it. But the bombs still fell, and those that were not dropped on strategic targets often fell on civilian ones instead. Throughout the last months of 1940 and well into 1941, all Britain's major cities were subjected to a remorseless pounding by Germany's bombers. But on the direct orders of Adolf Hitler himself, London suffered the full force of the Luftwaffe's unwavering wrath.

The London Blitz

The first heavy bombing raid on London came on 7 September 1940, when 300 bombers escorted by 600 fighters rumbled over the capital and dropped their deadly payloads with a great deal of success. Fighter Command had been severely weakened by the Battle of Britain, and the Luftwaffe were able to inflict significant damage on London's vital docks – as well as killing over 400 people. Hitler and Göring were greatly satisfied by the results of the raid, and similar attacks were ordered to continue. 7 September was the first of 58 nights of consecutive bombing attacks on London. With inadequate numbers of air raid shelters, the people of London took to sheltering in underground stations. Conditions were cramped and uncomfortable; there was little water and no sanitation. It was little better for those who hastily dug Anderson Shelters in their gardens, or hid themselves trembling in their basements.

Every night, for two months, the sound of air raid sirens heralded a new assault that the people of London knew would bring death and devastation to their city. Somehow the famous dome of St Paul's Cathedral managed to evade destruction, and for many it became a symbol of Churchill's defiant message that 'London can take it'. Each morning, pathways amidst the rubble were cleared and people attempted to go about their business as best they could.

> ## "A great world empire will be destroyed..."

We heard the weirdest sound like a whistling whine growing louder and louder and suddenly a terrific thud and explosion ... We grabbed our gas masks, knitting, books, coat and whatnot, and before we could get to the shelter two more screaming bombs fell, followed by an explosion, each one louder than the last ... Meanwhile the guns were booming nearby ... Bombs fell all around, the sky was alight as day with the fire and guns and planes. It was frightful. One of the bombs fell very, very close and the walls of the shelter shook. The woman I was sitting next to fainted in my arms, and I felt as sick as a dog ... It all seemed like a horrible nightmare. There's hardly a district in London that the Jerry's missed ... God we pray that they'd stay away but we know it's silly as Hitler said he'll blow London to bits. I'm a darned coward now, but I am hoping if a bomb does fall that we will be blown to bits and not get buried alive in the debris. Wouldn't it be terrible?

London resident, during the bombing campaign of the London Blitz, September 1940

The Coventry Blitz

Many other British cities suffered a similar fate to London, and one in particular was to endure such savage destruction that Hitler himself coined a new verb to describe it: 'Coventrize'.

On the evening of 14 November 1940, over 500 German bombers attacked Coventry, an industrial city in the English Midlands. It was poorly defended, and British attempts to jam the bombers' navigational radio signals failed. The bombs fell in the heart of the city, destroying its magnificent medieval cathedral and reducing huge swathes of housing to rubble. Its inhabitants crouched in the basements of nearby department stores, or fled to the surrounding countryside, sleeping in their cars or in the buildings of local farmers.

Although industrial production capacity returned very quickly to full strength, the Coventry Blitz had a lasting psychological and propaganda significance. The British used the attack on Coventry to highlight the barbarity of the Germans, and to galvanize public opinion rapidly to resist the Nazi war machine whatever the cost.

The so-called 'Blitz Spirit' of the British people led Hitler to conclude that the bombing raids were not having the desired effect of damaging British morale. The continued effectiveness of the RAF, and British victory in the Battle of the Beams meant that Luftwaffe losses were unsustainably high and ultimately Hitler postponed all thought of conquering the British Isles, and instead turned his forces to the east and the growing threat of the Soviet Union's Red Army.

A Promise to Avenge the Devastation

The Blitz is generally considered to have ended in mid-May 1941. Throughout this period, the Luftwaffe dropped over 35,000 tons of bombs on Britain. Well over 43,000 Britons were killed as a result. Many famous buildings in London were destroyed or badly damaged. But Britain remained defiant, and as the Germans turned their destructive power away from British cities towards Russia, Prime Minister Winston Churchill promised to avenge the destruction.

> *From now on we shall bomb Germany on an ever-increasing scale, month by month, year by year, until the Nazi regime has either been exterminated by us or — better still — torn to pieces by the German people themselves.*
>
> *British Prime Minister*
> *Winston S. Churchill*
> *Westminster, London 1941*

" ... Hitler said he'll blow London to bits ..."

Winston Churchill inspecting bomb damage in the Houses of Parliament, London.

Focke=Wulf Fw 190

Initially, the Focke-Wulf Fw 190 was the plane that nobody wanted. The Bf 109 had looked invincible. But the Battle of Britain in 1940 showed the Bf 109 did have vulnerabilities and in August 1941 the Fw 190 took to the skies for the first time operationally over France and went on to prove itself to be Germany's most versatile aircraft. The main reason the Fw 190 was commissioned was as a back-up to the much vaunted Bf 109. Focke-Wulf's plane used a BMW radial engine rather than the already much in-demand Daimler Benz unit used in the Messerschmitt.

Radial engines were seen as an inferior choice for fighter planes compared to inline engines as they impacted adversely on aerodynamics, but as the Fw 190 demonstrated, the extra horse power they could generate was ample compensation. The plane was consciously designed to allow numerous small sub-contractors to contribute to its production, meaning that no large factories would present easy targets for Allied bombers. By the end of the war Fw 190s were sourced from 24 different points of manufacture.

Heavier but stronger than Bf 109, the Fw 190 divided pilot opinion, but many German Flying Aces preferred Kurt Tank's Focke-Wulf design to the Messerschmitt, particularly at lower altitudes. German Aces Otto Kittel, Walter Nowotny and Erich Rudorffer all flew the Fw 190 and scored over 200 kills each. When tested by the RAF against early models of their frontline fighter, the Spitfire, an official report in 1942 concluded that the Fw 190 was superior in everything except turning circle.

No higher compliment could be paid to the Fw 190, and it saw service throughout World War II benefiting from constant improvement, particularly with regards to its performance at high altitude. Over 20,000 planes were produced, and in the opinion of many of the pilots, it was the Luftwaffe's greatest fighter of WWII.

THE DAMBUSTERS RAID

DATELINE ... 16 MAY 1943 ... 17 MAY 1943

Early in 1942, a British engineer by the name of Barnes Wallis was skimming marbles across water tanks in his garden. In his mind's eye he imagined them as bombs, skipping across the surface of a body of water to strike directly against a distant target. The idea of a 'bouncing bomb' would probably have been dismissed as an eccentric's flight of fancy had it been anyone else's proposal. But Barnes Wallis had a brilliant track record, having designed the inspired geodesic airframe of the Wellington bomber.

Operation Chastise

A bomb that could bounce on water would have two distinct advantages. Firstly it could evade torpedo nets, and secondly it could be launched in such a way as to detonate right against a target rather than in proximity to it. This was crucial when attacking certain highly robust targets, such as dam walls. Standard bombs were almost useless in such circumstances as it would require around 14 tons of explosives to destroy a dam, and no RAF bomber was capable of carrying such a load. Placed directly against a wall, however, just 3 tons of explosives would do the job.

Testing the new bomb was sanctioned, and it transpired that Wallis' concept was fundamentally sound. The bomb's shape was changed from spherical to cylindrical, and a way was found to deploy the bomb with backspin so that it would trail behind the bomber and allow the pilot to get clear of the area before it exploded. All that remained was to try it for real.

The dams of the Ruhr valley in northern Germany, were the logical target, providing, as they did, hydro-electric power and pure water for steel-making as well as drinking water, and water for Germany's canal transport system. Spring was the preferred time to strike, as the water levels in the dams would then be at their highest. It was believed a successful strike against them might cripple German industry for many months. The Ruhr was heavily defended, however, and the raid would therefore be incredibly risky.

The RAF's newly formed 617 Squadron of No. 5 Group was given the difficult task of delivering Barnes Wallis' bombs. It took to the air on 16 May 1943; a night of a full moon to give it the best possible chance of pinpointing the targets. Nineteen modified Lancaster bombers took part in the raid. The nine aircraft of Formation 1 were to attack the Möhne dam and, if they had any bombs remaining, proceed to attack the Eder dam after.

The five aircraft of Formation 2 were to attack the Sorpe dam, and the five aircraft of Formation 3 were to constitute a 'flying reserve' which would bomb any dams if they remained intact at the end. The main dams of Möhne and Sorpe contained around 70% of the water supplied to the Ruhr basin, and were thus the chief focus of the raid.

(Right) Destruction of Möhne Reservoir Dam.

The Bouncing Bombs

The formations took two different routes to reach their targets, each avoiding known concentrations of German anti-aircraft batteries. The pilots flew at a very low level in order to avoid detection by radar. Despite this, both formations soon ran into trouble. One aircraft of Formation 2 lost its radio to flak and had to turn back, another struck the sea and despite recovering was also obliged to return to base. Flak over the Dutch coast accounted for another Lancaster and a further one was lost after striking an electricity pylon near Haldern. The same fate befell one of the Lancasters of Formation 1, which otherwise managed to reach the targets unscathed. Formation 1 were first to attack, flying along the moonlit lake through heavy flak to strike at the Möhne dam.

The gunners had seen us coming. They could see us coming with our spotlights on from over two miles away. Now they opened up and the tracers came swirling towards us; some were even bouncing off the smooth surface of the lake. This was a horrible moment: we were being dragged along at four miles a minute, almost against our will, towards the things we were going to destroy. I think at that moment the boys did not want to go. I know I did not want to go. I thought to myself, 'In another minute we shall all be dead … so what?' I thought again, 'This is terrible – this feeling of fear – if it is fear.' By now we were a few hundred yards away, and I said quickly to Pulford, under my breath, 'Better leave the throttles open now and stand by to pull me out of the seat if I get hit.' As I glanced at him I thought he looked a little glum on hearing this … There was something sinister and slightly unnerving about the whole operation. My aircraft was so small and the dam was so large; it was thick and solid, and now it was angry. My aircraft was very small. We skimmed along the surface of the lake, and as we went my gunner was firing into the defences, and the defences were firing back with vigour, their shells whistling past us. For some reason, we were not being hit.

Wing Commander Guy Gibson
RAF Squadron 617, The Dambusters

The Dam Busters

Gibson's plane scored a perfect strike, and escaped safely. Others followed along the same treacherous flight path. Wallis' bombs performed as expected, and water poured through the breached dam to flood the valley below. One Lancaster was shot down and one damaged in the attack. Wing Commander Gibson then led the planes in an attack on the Eder dam. The first bomb dropped struck the top of the dam and the explosion severely damaged the unfortunate bomber. A second attack scored a direct hit, and was followed by a third attack which also managed to bomb the target. As a result, the Eder too, was breached.

Things went less well at the Sorpe dam, which was attacked by the single Lancaster that remained from Formation 2. It was an earthen dam, unlike the concrete dams at Möhne and Eder, and thus was always likely to be harder to destroy. The approach was difficult due to the need for the bombers to pull up hard to avoid hitting a hillside at the other end of the dam. Fog was also descending. It took the first attacking plane ten attempts to release its bomb at the correct moment and still avoid the hill. The bomb struck home but did not do as much damage as was hoped.

Three of the 'flying reserve' were called in to make further attacks, but one was shot down en route. The other two encountered heavy fog which made bombing accurately almost impossible. One bomber missed its target and the other aborted its bombing run entirely. The last two bombers of the 'flying reserve' were redirected to the smaller Lister and Ennepe dams. One was shot down before reaching the Lister and the last plane attacked the Ennepe but failed to hit the target.

Massive Morale Booster

Heavy flak on the return journey claimed another two Lancasters, meaning just nine of the original 19 returned home safely. The cost was equally high in human terms: 53 of the 113 airmen who participated in the attack were killed. On the ground in the Ruhr valley, it is estimated the floods caused by the attacks killed 1,650 people, most of them prisoners of war and workers. The damage to the Möhne dam caused significant disruption to German industry, but only for a matter of weeks, rather than the months or years that the British had hoped for. Repairs were urgently carried out, and Bomber Command flew no further raids to disrupt them.

The daring raid did, however, provide a major boost to morale in Britain, and the pilots of 'The Dambusters' became national heroes. Wing Commander Gibson was awarded the Victoria Cross for leading the raid. It also helped alleviate Stalin's concern that Britain was failing to help the Soviet Union by attacking Germany and her supply lines.

For the rest of World War II the dams were heavily defended, which drew an estimated 10,000 German troops away from the front-line. For the most part, these troops would essentially do nothing, and thus it could be argued that simply by demonstrating that Barnes Wallis' weapons worked, the Dambusters raid was highly successful in removing thousands of German troops from the war.

THE GLORIOUS DAM-BUSTER
GUY GIBSON

By the time Gibson was 24 years old he had completed 170 flying missions. He flew his first Lancaster in May 1942 as Wing Commander of 106 Squadron at RAF Coningsby. In November 1942 Gibson was awarded the DSO after bombing raids on Le Creusot and Montchanin in France and on Italian targets in Genoa, Milan and Turin. Commander-in-Chief of Bomber Command Arthur Harris nominated Gibson to lead Operation Chastise, the low level attacks on the dams in the Ruhr valley.

Gibson was awarded a VC after the raid and became something of a star, attending press conferences and accompanying Winston Churchill and Lord Mountbatten on a prestigious tour of Canada and America. He met President Roosevelt and revealed that Churchill had given him the nickname 'Dam-buster'. Harris wrote in July 1944 that the Americans had 'spoiled young Gibson' as the tour had 'gone to his head'.

On 19 September 1944, Guy Gibson was 26 years old when he flew his final bombing raid. His plane crashed at Steenbergen in the Netherlands. The cause of the crash has never been successfully explained and has remained a mystery for many years. Although members of his squadron have always maintained he simply ran out of fuel, a recent theory has emerged that he may have been shot down by friendly fire. Gibson's death was made official on 8 January 1945 and he received numerous posthumous tributes. Barnes Wallis said that Gibson was 'a man born for war … but born to fall in war'. While Churchill wrote: 'I had great admiration for him — the glorious Dam-buster. His name will not be forgotten.'

(Above) Wing Commander Guy Gibson; (below) King George VI inspects The Dambusters.

AVRO TYPE 683 LANCASTER

The backbone of RAF Bomber Command, the Avro Type 683 or 'Lancaster' bomber flew greater bomb loads further than any other bomber during World War II. Well over 7,000 were built, flying 156,000 sorties and dropping 600,000 tons of bombs.

The design evolved from the twin-engined Avro Manchester, in response to an Air Ministry specification for a new heavy bomber that could fly long distances carrying large loads at high speeds. Bomber Command had decided to use exclusively four-engined bombers despite the fact that four-engined bombers had yet to prove themselves, on the basis that twin-engined bombers were too vulnerable to flak and engine failure.

The first Lancasters entered service in late 1941, with four Merlin XX engines providing the power. The plane had a top speed of 270 mph, and could carry 14,000 pounds (6,350 kg) of bombs a distance of 1,160 miles (1,860 km). Two .303 Browning machine guns were in the nose and mid-turret positions, combined with four Brownings in the tail which provided rear cover. It had a wing span of 102 ft (31 m) and a length of over 69 ft (21 m). No German bomber could compare in terms of ability to deliver huge payloads over vast distances, and this would prove to be a decisive advantage to the Allied side in the course of World War II.

THE PLOESTI RAID

DATELINE ... I AUGUST 1943

Just as soldiers must eat so machines need fuel, and the Allies realized early on that German planes and tanks were ravenous for oil. Less than a month after the Pearl Harbor attack, the United States had drawn up a plan for attacking the Ploesti oil refinery in Romania. The British and Soviets had identified the same target and the latter had twice bombed Ploesti in 1941 and 1942, but had failed to cause significant damage. It was hardly surprising that the giant refinery near Bucharest was considered such a tempting target: the 9 million tons per year that flowed from Ploesti represented 60% of all Axis crude oil supplies. The problem was that Ploesti was heavily defended and difficult to reach from the British Isles. Any operation to attack the refinery would be complex logistically and would almost inevitably result in massive losses. But such was Ploesti's importance that it was decided an attack had to be attempted, and when the Allies made gains in North Africa it was felt that heavy bombers could at last be spared for the raid. Romania was just within range of USAAF bombers flying from bases in Libya and Syria.

Major-General Brereton, commander of the Ninth Air Force, was given the unenviable job of formulating a plan. A previous US attempt at bombing Ploesti in 1942 had been unsuccessful after the crews failed to locate their target. That mission was flown in darkness, and it was generally accepted that even if they had found the refinery they would not have achieved the accuracy required to badly damage it. So Brereton ruled out another night attack.

The Danger of Daylight

A high level attack would leave the bombers less vulnerable to flak, but would lose them the advantage of surprise. German radar would pick them up miles from their target, and Luftwaffe fighters would be sent to intercept them in large numbers. The German air force had become increasingly adept at mounting such operations against their attackers, using twin-engined fighters along with Focke-Wulf Fw 190s fitted with heavier guns to bring maximum firepower to bear against the well armoured bombers. The Allies were short of long-range fighters: Operation Torch had swallowed most available P-38s, and the P-47s equipped with extra fuel tanks that were due to be delivered were delayed by design problems. There was no choice for Brereton, then: the B-24 Liberators tasked with bombing Ploesti would fly unescorted, at low level, and in daylight. It was an incredibly dangerous mission, and Brereton knew it. He told his crew that he expected their losses to be around 50%, but assured them that even if that figure rose to 100% the mission would still be worthwhile, as long as they destroyed their target.

How the crew in question reacted to this assessment is not recorded. There were 1,725 Americans and one Englishman, with 178 planes to fly over 2,000 miles (3,200 km) to strike at Ploesti and back to base. Three groups of bombers were brought in from the Eighth Air Force in the United Kingdom to fly under Brereton's command. The B-24 Liberator was the only plane that had the required range to take them to Romania, but it was notorious for bursting into flames when hit due to its lightweight construction and the placement of fuel tanks in its upper fuselage. Powered by four 1,200 hp Pratt & Whitney radial engines it had a top speed of 290 mph, and for this particular mission the men relied on that rather than its ten .50 calibre M2 Browning machine guns for their primary defence.

Operation Tidal Wave

Seven separate targets were assigned to the forces involved in the attack: White I, II, III, IV and V were the main Ploesti targets and Blue and Red were targets at Brazi and Campina respectively. The bombsights in the B-24s were switched from the standard high-level sights to specially designed low-level modified gunsights. The planes would drop a mixture of 1,000 lb (450 kg) and 500 lb (225 kg) demolition bombs, plus a variety of British-made and American-made incendiaries. The bombs had delay fuses which ranged from 45 seconds to six hours. The crews began to train for the mission by attacking a dummy refinery laid out in the remote African desert as target practice. Eventually the bombers could completely destroy the target in under two minutes. They were ready to go. Operation Tidal Wave was launched just after dawn on 1 August 1943.

Almost immediately the mission suffered its first setbacks. One plane suffered engine failure on take-off and crash-landed back at the airfield, killing all but two of its crew.

Eleven further planes were forced to turn back for various technical reasons. The rest gathered around the lead aircraft and flew without incident for two and a half hours when, without warning or explanation, the lead aircraft suddenly dropped out of the sky and smashed into the sea. All of the planes were observing strict radio silence and could only communicate their horror and confusion by lamp lights. Eventually a new lead aircraft moved into position, but by the time the formations approached the coast of Yugoslavia low cloud made navigation difficult and the bombers lost sight of one another.

Two leading groups of planes took a railway leading south from the town of Targoviste to be their turning point, and headed away from Ploesti towards Bucharest. By the time they realized their mistake it was too late: Bucharest was the headquarters of Romanian defences and flak batteries across the country were soon alerted to the presence of enemy aircraft. The crew decided to break radio silence and warn the rest of the formation, though in truth there was little anyone could do. The two groups of planes above Bucharest decided to turn and attack Ploesti rather than abort their mission, but they would now be approaching from a completely different direction to the one they had so meticulously practised.

With the flak batteries forewarned and the bombers now arriving at different times and from different directions, the stage was set for carnage in the skies above Ploesti. The anti-aircraft fire was so ferocious that many bombers had to settle for striking any target that presented itself, dropping their payloads across a wide area rather than with precision. Many were blown from the sky before they could even reach their designated target. Bombs which did strike their targets caused fire and smoke to fill the sky, which meant the bombers who came later could hardly see. Balloon cables and chimneys became impossible to spot, but the B-24s flew on through the deadly obstacle course rather than turn back. Bomber Pilot Philip Ardery gave this account of the scene:

We found ourselves at that moment running a gauntlet of tracers and cannon fire of all types that made me despair of ever covering those last few hundred yards to the point where we could let the bombs go. The anti-aircraft defenses were literally throwing up a curtain of steel. From the target grew the column of flames, smoke, and explosions, and we were headed straight into it.

Ardery somehow managed to make it out, but all around him his colleagues were crashing to earth or bursting into flames:

I could feel tears come into my eyes and my throat clog up. Then I saw Pete pull up and out of formation. His bombs were laid squarely on the target along with ours. With his mission accomplished, he was making a valiant attempt to kill his excess speed and set the ship down in a little river valley south of the town before the whole business blew up. He was going about 210 miles per hour and had to slow up to about 110 to get the ship down. He was gliding without power, as it seemed, slowing up and pulling off to the right in the direction of a moderately flat valley: Pete was fighting now to save himself and his men. He was too low for any of them to jump and there was not time for the airplane to climb to a sufficient altitude to permit a chute to open. The lives of the crew were in their pilot's hands, and he gave it everything he had. Wells, in our waist gun compartment, was taking pictures of the gruesome spectacle. Slowly the ship on our right lost speed and began to settle in a glide that looked like it might come to a reasonably good crash-landing. But flames were spreading furiously all over the left side of the ship. I could see it plainly, as it was on my side. Now it would touch down — but just before it did, the left wing came off. The flames had been too much and had literally burnt the wing off. The heavy ship cartwheeled and a great shower of flame and smoke appeared just ahead of the point where last we had seen a bomber.

As the survivors turned for home they had to gain height in order to cross the mountains. They did so just as the Luftwaffe fighters arrived. At lower levels the bombers were hard to engage, but once higher up the bombers were desperately vulnerable to attack. Squadron after squadron of Bf 109s and Focke-Wulfs harassed the US formations, and the Romanian Air Force joined in the slaughter with their mixture of modern IAR-80 fighters and more antiquated planes. Even the Romanian Gloster Gladiator biplanes managed to score heavily, dropping fragmentation bombs on the B-24s which shattered their wings or tails. As the US pilots fought desperately to evade destruction they used far more fuel than anticipated, meaning that for many their home bases became out of range. Emergency landings were made by some in Turkey, others limped back to Malta, Sicily or Cyprus.

Black Sunday

The losses were horrific. Of the 178 Liberators originally dispatched, 166 managed to reach and attack Ploesti and the nearby refineries. Almost all of the planes that returned were damaged, and

53 Liberators failed to return at all. The total number of US dead stood at 440, with many more wounded and some 200 taken prisoner. The raid delivered a serious but not critical blow to Axis oil supplies; the Romanian refineries were still producing oil when Soviet forces overran them a year later. The raid was a disaster for the USAAF and became known as 'Black Sunday'.

Though mistakes were made in the air, the blame did not lie with the heroic air crews who took part in the mission. Five Medals of Honor were awarded to them – the largest number of America's highest award ever given for a single operation in World War II. The tragedy was caused by a mixture of poor planning and poor intelligence. Ground defences at Ploesti were even stronger than was realized, and the low-flying B-24s were easy targets. The fact that the flak batteries were given advance notice of the attack compounded the issue. The plan had failed to take into account the difficulty of keeping a large number of planes in formation over such a large distance, and relied too heavily on a single lead navigator plane successfully guiding all of the others to the target. Many of the bombs that were dropped on Ploesti failed to explode, and thus the crews' bravery counted for nothing.

But it was always going to be a dangerous and difficult mission, and such missions were vital if the war was to be won. The Ploesti raid failed terribly, but many other similar attacks were highly successful. Just two weeks after 'Black Sunday' the same five bomber groups were once again in action, and once again they flew over 1,000 miles (1,600 km) from North Africa deep into enemy territory. This time the target was Wiener Neustadt in

Austria, where a variety of the Luftwaffe's fighters and bombers were produced and repaired. The mistakes of Ploesti were not repeated, and the 65 bombers achieved total tactical surprise. Huge damage was caused to the assembly plants and hangars, and only light flak and a handful of enemy fighters were encountered. Whenever the Allied bomber crews climbed into their aircraft, they did not know whether they would be flying towards disaster or glory. But they continued to fly.

An American B-24 Liberator bomber during the attack on Ploesti, Romania.

B-24 Liberators flying through the destruction, after attacking the oil refinery at Ploesti, Romania.

THE D-DAY LANDINGS

DATELINE ... 6 JUNE 1944 ... 22 AUGUST 1944

Taking 850,000 men, 148,000 vehicles and well over 500,000 tons of supplies across the English Channel and landing them safely in France was never going to be easy. It required supreme logistical coordination between all sections of the combined Allied forces. D-Day – the Allied invasion of Nazi-occupied Normandy on 6 June 1944 – had to be a night of a full moon, as a clear, bright sky was absolutely key for the air forces. The day initially scheduled for the invasion, 5 June 1944, was cloudy with poor visibility, so General Dwight D. Eisenhower, Supreme Commander of the Allied Forces in Europe, decided to postpone the invasion. Clearer weather arrived the next day, 6 June 1944, and Eisenhower gave the green light for Operation Overlord. The Allied invasion of Europe had begun.

The Invasion of Normandy

The plan for Operation Overlord – the Allied invasion of Normandy – called for an amphibious assault on five beaches. The British and Canadians would team up to take Sword Beach in the east. The Canadians would take Juno Beach; the British Gold Beach, and the Americans would take Omaha Beach and Utah Beach to the west.

The only reason that the invasion was considered possible was due to Allied air superiority over France. Even Hitler had hesitated at the idea of attempting a massive amphibious assault without overwhelming air support. By the time the troops began to head across the channel, the RAF and

USAAF had already made a number of vital contributions to the mission. Rail and road communications were attacked to cut off the area marked for invasion. French ports which housed fast German Navy attack craft and U-boats were also targeted, as were ammunition and fuel dumps.

Three days before the invasion, 96 Lancasters and four Pathfinder Mosquitos had completely destroyed the HQ of the German Signals Intelligence Service near the port of Cherbourg. It would later be discovered that this was the Nazi's chief intelligence listening station in Normandy. On 4 June, 23 Spitfires attacked the Wurzburg radar station 13 miles west of the port of Le Havre on France's north-west coast. Nine direct hits were scored, putting the station out of action for the crucial invasion period.

The most telling damage, however, was that done to the Luftwaffe itself. In the early months of 1944 the Allies flew countless sorties that stretched the German air force to its limits, and eventually effectively broke it. 'Big Week', from 20 – 25 February 1944, was especially costly to the Luftwaffe in terms of fighter pilots. Heavily escorted bombing raids saw P-51 Mustangs engage ceaselessly with German fighters and while both sides suffered heavy losses the 100 experienced pilots lost by the Luftwaffe could not be replaced. The US was by now turning out new aircraft, and training new pilots, at a prodigious rate.

The Germans, now on the receiving

end of punishing attacks on their aircraft industry, could not come close to matching the Allied production levels. Even if they had been able to, there were too few pilots to fly the planes. Between January and June 1944 the Luftwaffe lost 2,262 pilots. As the Allied air forces turned the screw ahead of D-Day, the Luftwaffe's operational losses in May climbed to a staggering 50%. Little wonder, then, that the German air force could contribute less than a hundred sorties while defending Normandy.

The Onslaught Unleashed

Throughout the week leading up to D-Day, Allied aircraft made a number of 'deception sorties' on coastal batteries around the port of Calais to convince the Germans that this was where the Allies planned to land their invasion force. On the night before D-Day, 259 aircraft took part in one particularly large deception raid, but this time they were also tasked with striking a 'real' target, the Maisy Battery which lay between 'Omaha' and 'Utah' beaches. Heavy cloud prevented them from striking the target accurately. It was a failure that would cost many Allied troops their lives when the invasion of Normandy began.

RAF Bomber Command committed 82 squadrons to assisting Operation Neptune, the code name designating the amphibious landing itself. Virtually all of its 1,681 serviceable aircraft were concentrated on supporting the main assault and the beachhead. Planes from the Allied Expeditionary Air Force were used to transport troops and supplies, and to provide fighter cover and reconnaissance.

The 2nd Tactical Air Force (TAF) consisted of 33 fighter squadrons, 18 fighter-bomber squadrons, 12 light bomber squadrons and 17 reconnaissance and artillery observation squadrons. Attached to the 2nd TAF were many of the exiled pilots who had fled to Britain after their homelands

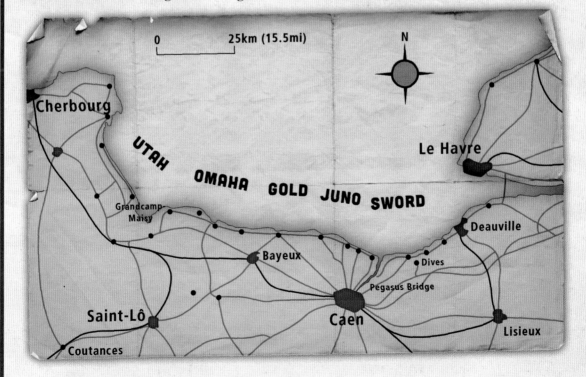

Map of the Normandy coastline showing the Allied invasion beaches.

were invaded and Free French pilots were more than enthusiastic volunteers in the liberation of France.

At 21:30 on 5 June 1944, we assembled in the Ops Room and learned that tomorrow was to be Jour J. Our Wing, No 145 of 2TAF, Ops officer uncovered the wall map and we were amazed by what we saw. This news, so long awaited by all the pilots, aroused huge delight. Our hopes during four years of waiting were about to be realized: at last to see our families and tread our native soil again. This time the invasion was on. On the map, arrows made long tracks across the Channel from the Isle of Wight to the Normandy coast. The onslaught had been unleashed. It was difficult to close one's eyes that night.

We flew twice that day over the landing beaches. The first time we took off in the morning we saw that for 180 km an immense convoy of vessels crowded the sea. Thousands of aircraft filled the sky and we had to keep a sharp lookout for them as well as keep formation. Christian Martell, who led the wing, had warned us at the briefing: 'I don't want to see pilots watching the ground. Today you've got to scan the sky.'

But the sky remained void of enemy aircraft that morning, at least for us. We were covering General Crerar's First Canadian Army on Sword and Juno Beaches. The only danger was of collision with the other aircraft in a small, crowded airspace. The air umbrella was indeed up.

Anonymous Pilot, Free French Air Force

The Strain of Imminent Invasion

US air forces were divided along similar lines, with the USAAF's Eighth Air Force teaming up with RAF Bomber Command, and the USAAF's Ninth Air Force working with 2nd TAF under the overall control of Air Chief Marshal Sir Trafford Leigh-Mallory. The US Ninth Air Force consisted of several commands, providing tactical support for the First and Third armies.

The relationship between the RAF and USAAF, which had until this date been so close, began to break down under the strain of the imminent invasion. Indeed, frustrating cracks began to appear in the relationships between the commanders of the respective air forces and the commanders of the ground forces. US British rivalries were also taken to their limits.

General Bernard Montgomery, commander of the land forces on D-Day, was once again facing an old German adversary, 'The Desert Fox' Field Marshal Erwin Rommel, charged with defending the beaches at Normandy. Montgomery had been criticized for not pursuing Rommel's retreating forces more vigorously after the Battle of El Alamein in North Africa in 1942, and some critics in the combined air forces feared he would make a similar mistake during the Normandy invasion.

The air force wanted Montgomery to push as quickly as possible towards key German airfields so that Allied pilots would not have to operate across the Channel from bases in Britain. Dogged and determined, Montgomery was not a risk taker and he focused instead on ensuring the success of the landings. His priorities lay with defeating Rommel's tanks.

Montgomery's advance towards the German airfields was even slower than planned. He had aimed to take Caen on the first day. The city did not fall until 6 August 1944, two months later. But ultimately it did not matter because the Allied air forces had been even more successful than they realized in the months leading up to D-Day. They had established not just air superiority, but complete air supremacy.

Operation Neptune
The Beach Landings

Air commanders had warned the ground commanders that it would be difficult to destroy the well-defended and well-concealed German positions above the landing beaches, and so it proved. At Omaha Beach in particular, the resistance met by the invading Allied troops was fierce. Despite repeated heavy bombing by the Eighth Air Force during the early hours of 6 June 1944, many of the main gun emplacements remained intact. A huge naval bombardment preceded the landings, but even this could not strike with the repeated accuracy required to destroy the German positions. Fighter-bombers were brought in to support the troops and had some success, but often they dropped their ordnance too far inland for fear of striking the landing craft. The 1st and 29th divisions had to fight every inch of the way at Omaha and as a result casualties were high: 2,000 men were killed or wounded.

On D-Day itself, 171 squadrons of British and USAAF fighters flew a variety of sorties in support of the invasion. Fifty-four squadrons provided beach cover, 33 undertook bomber escort missions, 15 provided shipping cover, 33 attacked inland targets and 36 provided tactical air support to the invasion forces. Offensive fighter sweeps were undertaken in the expectation that the skies would soon fill with Luftwaffe Messerschmitt Bf 109s and Focke-Wulf Fw 190s. Very few German fighters arrived, however, and those that did were hopelessly outnumbered and quickly dealt with.

Hitler was delighted when he heard of the Allied assault. 'The news could not be better,' he said. 'As long as they were in Britain we couldn't get at them. Now we have them where we can destroy them.'

On 12 June 1944, the American and British beachheads were finally joined, making a long thin enclave 60 miles (96 km) long and 15 miles (24 km) deep. Then an American thrust by General Joseph 'Lightin Joe' Collins across the Cotentin peninsula cut off Cherbourg. Another push created a 20-mile (32 km) salient to the south. By 18 June, there were 600,000 men ashore, while German formations were being destroyed by planes flying from airstrips hastily constructed inside the beachhead.

Audacious Airborne Assault

Although D-Day was largely a seaborne operation, airborne troops were sent in first to disrupt the German defenders. British paratroopers were dropped over France by Armstrong Whitworth Albemarle transport planes, with others flying in via Airspeed AS.51 Horsa gliders, tasked with capturing the bridges over the Caen Canal and River Orne. Tactically and strategically significant, the canal connected the city of Caen to the English Channel. Around 13,000 US paratroopers were followed by almost 4,000 glider troops in an assault designed to capture causeway exits off the beaches and establish crossings over the Douvre river. Both of these airborne assaults were carried out at night, making them highly dangerous for the troops involved.

NORTH AMERICAN AVIATION
P-51 MUSTANG

Pilots who flew the P-51 fighter bomber shot down 4,950 enemy planes during World War II, though it was initially flown for long-range tactical and strategic reconnaissance purposes. It was the RAF that commissioned the plane after initially approaching North American Aviation (NAA) about the possibility of manufacturing the Curtiss P-40 Tomahawk under license, as Curtiss themselves were running close to capacity. NAA's President 'Dutch' Kindelberger offered to build a brand new aircraft instead, and the P-51 was born.

The first prototype of what was then called the NA-73X flew on 26 October 1940, just 149 days after the RAF order had been placed. It performed almost faultlessly. Relatively simple and inexpensive to build, the P-51 used a version of the already proven and reliable Rolls Royce Merlin engine and had plenty of interior space for large fuel tanks.

The P-51's long range made it immensely flexible, and particularly well suited for supporting heavy bombers on raids deep into enemy territory. Six .50 calibre M2 Browning machine guns provided plenty of fire power, and the plane also performed admirably when used as a fighter-bomber. The Mustang could not match the Spitfire or Messerschmitt Bf 109 in a one-on-one dogfight, but in the wider context of the battle for air superiority over Europe, the versatility of the P-51 proved decisive in the ultimate Allied victory.

The British troops suffered heavy losses but achieved all of their objectives by the end of 6 June 1944. The American troops did not fare so well. Almost half of the units were dropped in the wrong location and small groups of paratroopers roamed the fields of France looking for their divisions. The chaotic nature of the attack, however, served to confuse the German defenders who could not work out where the American forces were concentrated or what their ultimate target might be.

Further drops during daylight had to contend with heavy flak, but at least served to reinforce the fragmented US positions. Again, the absence of Luftwaffe fighters meant that fewer troops were lost during the drops than was feared, although heavy pockets of resistance on the ground cost many lives.

Delays in taking key strategic targets also proved costly for the troops wading ashore onto the beaches. However the losses sustained never placed the operation in real jeopardy, proving once again the vital advantage of air supremacy.

Rapid Response Raiders

The 'cab rank' style of stacking circling air-assault aircraft developed by the Desert Air Force in North Africa was used during Operation Overlord and refinements in radar made it even more effective. Each Air-Ground Coordination Party requesting air support would be able to give precise locations as each had its own mobile radar. Fighter-bombers already in the air and waiting instructions could then be rapidly guided to the scene. Radar helped enormously in avoiding 'friendly fire' incidents by locating where hostile and

friendly troop positions lay. Swift air attacks were especially useful in preventing German forces from retreating and taking up new positions. Air reconnaissance in turn gave the ground commanders vital information about the exact locations of enemy positions and their relative strength.

Despite all the fractious disagreements between the air and ground forces ahead of the invasion, once the invasion was underway they cooperated closely. The result was that the Germans could not resist the massive combined assault. Except for an attack in the Calais area, many local German commanders failed to react fast enough to the Normandy assault.

Communication breakdowns exacerbated the problem. Rommel himself was on leave on the morning of the invasion, and could not personally coordinate the response. German Panzer reserves were not committed, in case they were needed for the expected larger 'deception' attack further north at Calais.

By the end of D-Day, around 150,000 troops had successfully landed in Normandy. Rommel whose strategy had largely relied on denying the Allies any kind of initial foothold on the beaches, knew that, having now achieved a landing, stopping the Allied advance would be almost impossible.

The Battle of Normandy

The countryside of northern France, with its high hedgerows and narrow lanes, made Allied progress dangerous and difficult. Though the initial beach landings were considered a great success, the weeks that followed saw the invasion falter badly. In particular the failure of American troops to capture the vital port of Cherbourg on the Cotentin peninsula in north-western France,

American B-26 Marauder flying over Sword beach on D-Day 1944.

was a serious blow, as the Allies still had no deep water port to land supplies.

Cherbourg eventually fell on 26 June 1944, but the retreating German commander destroyed all the port's facilities, rendering it inoperable. The British fared even worse in their attempt to take Caen, 75 miles (120 km) to the east. A bloody stalemate evolved, and a strong German counter-attack threatened to reverse Montgomery's hard-won gains until heavy bombing of the city finally broke German resistance.

It rained heavily throughout July and the fighting became – literally – bogged down.

The RAF dropped 2,500 tons of bombs on Caen. After two days of fighting, the British took the north-western part of the city at the cost of 3,500 casualties.

A massive attack was then prepared on German positions to the east and south of Caen. This was called Operation Goodwood. On the eve of the advance, Rommel was machine-gunned in his staff car by an RAF fighter. He took no further part in the fighting and committed suicide while convalescing after being implicated in the July assassination plot to kill Hitler.

Operation Cobra

The Americans planned to breakout to the south and south-east from the beaches of Normandy. For Operation Cobra to succeed they needed the leadership of a military genius. Fortunately, the Americans had just such a man – General George S. Patton, nicknamed 'Old Blood and Guts' by his men.

Patton had landed on Utah beach on 6 July without even getting his feet wet. US forces fought their way to the town of Coutances in north-western France, 50 miles (80 km) south of Cherbourg. On 25 July, 3,000 USAAF bombers dropped 4,000 tons of high-explosive, fragmentation and napalm bombs on a five-mile stretch of the German front to the west of St-Lô.

The first line had been annihilated by the bombing ... The three-hour bombardment on the 25th – after the smaller one a day before – had an exterminating morale effect on the troops physically and morally weakened by continual hard fighting for 45 days. The long duration of the bombing, without any possibility for opposition, created depressions and a feeling of helplessness, weakness and inferiority. Therefore the morale attitude of a great number of men grew so bad that they, feeling the uselessness of fighting, surrendered, deserted to the enemy or escaped to the rear, as far as they survived the bombing.

Only particularly strong nerved and brave men could endure this strain. The shock effect was nearly as strong as the physical effect (dead and wounded). During the bombardment ... some of the men got crazy and were unable to carry out anything. I have been personally on the 24th and 25th in the center of the bombardment and could experience the tremendous effect. For me, who during this war was in every theater committed at the points of the main efforts, this was the worst I ever saw.

The well-dug-in infantry was smashed by the heavy bombs in their foxholes and dugouts or killed and buried by blast. The positions of infantry and artillery were blown up. The whole bombed area was transformed into fields covered with craters, in which no human being was alive. Tanks and guns were destroyed and overturned and could not be recovered, because all roads and passages were blocked ...

Generalleutnant Fritz Bayerlein
Panzer-Lehr-Division
Normandy, July 1944

The ruined town of Coutances, Normandy, July 1944.

PEGASUS BRIDGE

As part of the British airborne operation, the 6th Airborne Division was to take control of the area between the Rivers Orne and Dives to protect the flank of the seaborne landings from the German reserve forces that were massed to the east of Caen. They were to destroy the bridges over the Dives to prevent a German counter-attack and capture intact the bridges over the Orne and the Caen Canal — known by its codename Pegasus — so that reinforcements landing on the beaches could join up with the airborne assault.

The bridges were defended by some 50 men of the German 736th Grenadier Regiment, 716th Infantry Division, largely conscripts from Russia, Poland and France. Their commander, Major Hans Schmidt, had been told that the two bridges were the two most critical points in Normandy as they were the only crossing points of the Orne waterways along the coast road.

Although the invasion had long been anticipated, only two sentries were on guard that night. The rest of Schmidt's men were either sleeping in their bunker or dozing at their posts. Schmidt himself was with his girlfriend a mile away in Ranville. He had orders to blow up the bridges if capture seemed imminent. They had been prepared for demolition, but the explosives had not been put in place for fear of partisan reprisals.

As the bridges were almost five miles inland, Schmidt figured that he would have plenty of warning before any Allied troops could reach him and the explosives could be put in place then. Even if there was an airborne assault, paratroopers took time to form up and organize themselves once they had landed.

However, the attack on the bridges was not going to be made by amphibious troops or paras. The British assault troops were going to arrive in six Airspeed Horsa gliders. These were high-winged 67-ft (20 m) monoplanes with a 88-ft (26 m) wingspan. They would be towed over the English Channel by Halifax bombers, then released after they crossed the Normandy coast to glide silently towards their objective.

These 'silent coffins', as they were known, could carry 30 men, or a jeep and ten men. The six gliders used on Operation Deadstick — the raid on Pegasus Bridge — each carried a platoon from the 2nd (Airborne) Battalion, an assault boat, a mortar, a radio and five Royal Engineers to disarm the explosives they expected to find. They were led by Major John Howard. His men, some as young as 19 years old, sang as the gliders took off from England.

> " ... there was no going back ... "

They crossed the coast to the east of the River Orne and, at 00:07 hours, Staff Sergeant Jim Wallwork, pilot of the lead glider, codenamed Chalk 91, released the tow rope. The singing stopped as the drone of the bombers' engines faded. All that could be heard was the rush of air over the gliders' wings. Now there was no going back.

The Halifaxes were to go on to bomb a cement factory in Caen as a diversion. From the release point, the glider had six or seven miles to cover to the target. This would take three-and-a-half minutes, which the co-pilot watched tick away on a stopwatch.

Sergeant Wallwork could recognize nothing on the ground, but when his co-pilot Staff Sergeant John Ainsworth indicated that the flight time had elapsed, he turned to starboard and dropped the flaps to bring the glider down from 7,000 to 500 ft (2,100 to 150 m). They were still flying at 110 mph and were to aim for a small triangular field 500 yards (450 m) long with its apex at the bridge. It was still nowhere in sight. Pathfinder paratroopers were supposed to have been dropped 1 hour and 40 minutes before the gliders arrived to mark out the landing zone with flares, but they had arrived only 5 minutes earlier and no lights could be seen.

Then Ainsworth spotted the bridge. Wallwork called over his shoulder for Howard to get ready. The men had to link arms to stop themselves being thrown around and yell to prevent deafness from the rapidly changing air pressure. As they came into land, they had to raise their feet to avoid broken bones.

At 00:16 hours — just 16 minutes into D-Day — Chalk 91 crashed into the field. Its nose came to rest against the barbed-wire that surrounded the bridge. The sudden impact flung two pilots forward through the windscreen of the cockpit. The rest of the men were stunned by the jolt. Howard's seatbelt had snapped and he hit his head on the glider's roof. When he came round, he found he was blind — only temporarily — as his helmet had been forced down over his eyes.

The platoon commander, Lieutenant Herbert 'Denny' Brotheridge, had the door open and ordered the Bren-gunner, Private Billy Gray, out. The men then raced the 30 yards (27 m) to the bridge.

When a German appeared to the right of them, Gray gave him a burst with his Bren gun and saw him fall. Then he raced on over the bridge to the barn he had been designated to clear. Opening the door, he flung in a grenade, then emptied the rest of his magazine. But there was no one inside.

As Lieutenant Brotheridge led the rest of the men across the bridge, he pulled out a grenade and threw it at the machine-gun to his right. It had just left his hand when a bullet hit him in the neck. The grenade knocked out the machine gun as Brotheridge lay dying.

A minute later, the second Horsa, Chalk 92, came in at a steep angle. The parachute brake tipped it forward. As it hit the ground, it broke in two. Most of the men inside were injured and one was thrown into the canal and drowned.

Lieutenant David Wood was flung out of the glider carrying a canvas bucket full of grenades. None went off. The few uninjured men began clearing the remaining trenches and bunkers. Then the word 'Ham' and 'Jam' were broadcast over the radio. These were the code words signifying that the two bridges had been taken intact. They now had to hold them until amphibious troops, who would not start landing on the Normandy beaches until hours later, got there.

> ## "…It could take your leg off landing at 90 mph…"
> Lance Sergeant Raymond 'Tich' Raynor, 2nd Airborne Battalion

Glider Chalk 91 (center) piloted by Jim Wallwork, landed within feet of Pegasus Bridge, which can just be seen in the background.

Closing the Falaise Pocket

German commanders began to fear they would become encircled by the Allied advance. Their request to Hitler to withdraw to the Seine was over-ruled by the Führer who demanded a counter-attack instead. No one, with the exception of Hitler, had any faith in the plan. The commander of 116 Panther Division had to be replaced when he refused to join the attack.

Through Ultra, the military intelligence code breakers based at Bletchley Park in England, the Allies knew Hitler's plans. A stubborn man, he was not about to order a retreat. This left his entire army in Normandy liable to be encircled. While the British and Canadians pushed south-east and eastwards, cutting off his retreat to the Seine, Patton was told to turn northward, closing the trap.

On 16 August the Canadians reached Falaise. Patton was just 12 miles (20 km) to the south at Argentan. The German 7th Army and their Panzer support were now caught in a pocket. Patton begged Omar Bradley, the Commander-in-Chief of the American Ground Force for permission to close the gap, encircling the enemy. But Bradley refused, fearing that he did not have enough men in place to resist the counter-attack such a move was bound to provoke.

The Allies had made further landings in the South of France and Hitler, belatedly, gave permission for the 7th Army to withdraw. But it was too late. The Canadians pushed southwards, closing the Falaise gap to just a few hundred yards. Despite fierce fighting, on 20 August, it was closed altogether. Those left in the pocket were pulverized by Allied bombing. The stench of rotting flesh was so strong that those flying in planes overhead could smell it. Resistance ceased on 22 August 1944. Visiting the battlefield two days later, General Eisenhower said that you could walk on the dead for hundreds of yards on end. Upon hearing of the news, Hitler relieved Field Marshal Gunther von Kluge of his command and recalled him to Berlin. He committed suicide en route.

It was left to the new commander, Field Marshal Walter Model to arrange an orderly withdrawal. Forcing his way back towards Paris and the river Seine, Model met ferocious resistance from Allied forces, and in particular from Polish forces. They were attacked repeatedly by Allied aircraft, with RAF Typhoons proving especially deadly. P-51 Mustangs and Spitfires strafed the fleeing columns and provided invaluable reconnaissance of their every move.

Bearing the Colossal Consequences

Over a period of ten days some 20,000 – 50,000 German troops managed to escape, though large amounts of tanks and heavy artillery were abandoned in the rush and many more were destroyed by ground attack aircraft. It is believed 5,000 vehicles were destroyed in the first three days of the withdrawal. When the desperate troops reached the Seine they found that the Allies had destroyed the bridges. A bottleneck developed, which RAF and USAAF medium bombers attacked ruthlessly. Around 10,000 – 15,000 German troops were killed, and a further 50,000 taken prisoner. Although Allied leaders were frustrated at the number who evaded them, the battle at Falaise remained a disaster for Germany. It was one from which she would never fully recover. Paris was liberated two days later, and from there the Allied forces regrouped, and began the march to Berlin.

A Witness to History
Fritz Bayerlein

Born in Würzburg, Franconia, in Germany's heartland, Fritz Bayerlein joined the 9th Bavarian Infantry in 1917. When he was 18 years old, he fought on the Western Front during World War I. In World War II, he was driving a Panzer tank at the German invasion of Poland, the invasion of France and the invasion of Russia. He served with Rommel's *Afrika Korps* in Egypt and was at Tobruk and the Battle of El Alamein in 1942. In October 1943, he was sent to The Eastern Front to lead the 3rd Panzer Division and was later assigned to command the Panzer-Lehr-Division.

On 7 June 1944, Panzer-Lehr-Division were in Normandy and were obliterated by Allied carpet bombing attacks near St-Lô. Bayerlein lived to tell the tale, however, and was Commander of the 53rd Armee Korps when on 19 April 1945 he eventually surrendered along with over 30,000 German troops in the Ruhr Valley. The first of the war in Europe, this large surrender initiated the German disintegration and an end to the fighting, and Bayerlein became a prisoner of war until April 1947.

After being a first-hand witness at many of the most historic events of World War II, Fritz Bayerlein died, aged 71, in his home town of Würzburg. His death was due to a severe recurrent malarial disease contracted when he was in Egypt with the *Afrika Korps* in 1942. Many said that World War II had finally caught up with Fritz Bayerlein.

(Above) Fritz Bayerlein; (below left to right) Rommel, Bayerlein and Kesselring.

THE BOMBING OF DRESDEN

DATELINE ... 13 FEBRUARY 1945 ... 15 FEBRUARY 1945

The British Air Ministry's ultimate aim was to hasten the collapse of Germany by launching heavy bombing raids on Berlin, Dresden, Leipzig and Chemnitz. These targets all lay just behind the German lines at the Eastern Front and it was considered that an attack on them would prevent reinforcements arriving to halt the Soviet advance from the East. The Soviets had requested Allied assistance of this kind at the Yalta Conference in February, and had identified the railway junctions at Dresden as one particularly strategically significant target.

Operation Thunderclap

Dresden, the capital of the German state of Saxony, however, was more than simply a military target. 'The Florence of the Elbe' was considered to be one of Germany's most beautiful historic cities and a landmark of German culture. It had become a haven for refugees fleeing the Soviet advance. Given the chaotic nature of war, it will never be known how many such refugees were actually in the city at the time of the bombing, but the difficulty the German authorities would have in rehousing them was mentioned in an RAF memo to the crews as one of the key reasons for striking Dresden.

Dresden, the seventh largest city in Germany and not much smaller than Manchester is also the largest unbombed built up area the enemy has got. In the midst of winter with refugees pouring westward and troops to be rested, roofs are at a premium, not only to give shelter to workers, refugees, and troops alike, but to house the administrative services displaced from other areas. At one time well known for its china, Dresden has developed into an industrial city of first-class importance ... The intentions of the attack are to hit the enemy where he will feel it most, behind an already partially collapsed front ... and incidentally to show the Russians when they arrive what Bomber Command can do.

RAF Memo, February 1945
Briefing the attack on Dresden

The Decimation of Dresden

The city was attacked in four raids over several days by both the USAAF and RAF dropping more than 3,900 tons of high-explosive bombs and fire-starting incendiaries. But it was a single 63-minute attack by the RAF on the night of 13 February 1945 that caused the vast majority of deaths in the city. A bombing party of 529 Lancasters dropped more than 1,800 tons of bombs on Dresden. Aided in their task by clear weather and minimal flak from the city's few air defences this attack created a firestorm that destroyed 15 square miles (40 square km) of the city.

There were few public air-raid shelters, and fire-fighting provision in the city was woefully inadequate. An RAF assessment after the raid suggested that around 78,000 dwellings had been completely destroyed with a further 27,000 rendered uninhabitable and 64,000 damaged.

At the time, authorities in Dresden reported the death toll as being around 25,000, and a recent special German government commission appears to support this figure, with 20,100 victims known by name. However, the Nazi propaganda machine claimed that as many as 500,000 were incinerated by the blaze and many commentators believe that, given the large number of refugees in the vicinity, the official death toll underestimates the number of casualties.

The Final Futility of War

Dresden was the last major victim of the 'carpet bombing' strategy in Europe, with even Churchill himself at the end of March 1945 officially questioning the justification of such heavy bombing raids on targets with little military significance in a memo written to General Ismay for the British Chiefs of Staff and Chief of the Air Staff.

It seems to me that the moment has come when the question of bombing of German cities simply for the sake of increasing the terror, though under other pretexts, should be reviewed. Otherwise we shall come into control of an utterly ruined land ... The destruction of Dresden remains a serious query against the conduct of Allied bombing. I am of the opinion that military objectives must henceforward be more strictly studied in our own interests than that of the enemy. The Foreign Secretary has spoken to me on this subject, and I feel the need for more precise concentration upon military objectives such as oil and communications behind the immediate battle-zone, rather than on mere acts of terror and wanton destruction, however impressive.

British Prime Minister Winston S. Churchill
Memo to British Chiefs of Staff and
Chief of the Air Staff, 28 March 1945

Whatever the exact number of fatalities in Dresden, no one can doubt the horror of the bombing for those who endured it. One of those who survived the appalling devastation was the author Kurt Vonnegut, who was a prisoner of war in Dresden at the time. His satirical novel *Slaughterhouse 5* was inspired by the experience and is widely regarded as one of the finest books ever to have been written about the futility of war.

Less than a month after Churchill's memo was sent to the Chiefs of Staff, the Battle of Berlin began, and on 30 April 1945, with Soviet forces just 500 yards (500 m) from his bunker, Adolf Hitler committed suicide. Germany formally surrendered on 8 May 1945. World War II in Europe was over.

(Left) B-17 Flying Fortresses drop bombs on Dresden, 1945.

BOEING B-17 FLYING FORTRESS

Like the Lancaster, the B-17 'Flying Fortress' was a four-engined heavy bomber, used primarily in World War II during the bombing campaign against German cities. Introduced in 1938, the design was steadily improved upon during the war, but the basic concept of the plane was so successful that it remained the USAAF's main bomber until the Allied victory in 1945, dropping 640,000 tons of bombs by that time.

The first flight of a B-17 (then designated 'Model 299') was on 28 July 1935. Struck by the numerous machine gun installations in evidence on the plane, *Seattle Times* journalist Richard Williams described it as a

'flying fortress', and the name stuck. There were five 0.3 inch machine guns in total, including one in the nose of the plane that could rotate to repel enemy attack from almost any frontal angle. By the time the definitive B-17G appeared, the number of guns had risen to 13 — each being a .50 inch M2 Browning machine gun.

The B-17E could carry 4,500 lbs (2,040 kg) of bombs and had a range of 2,000 miles (3,200 km), with a service ceiling of 35,600 feet (10,850 m) and a maximum speed of 287 mph. It became legendary for its ability to withstand extraordinary levels of damage and still bring its crew of 10 home. Despite this, it was soon realized that the B-17 required fighter escorts when making the perilous journey across Nazi Germany. Numerous mechanical problems dogged early versions of the plane, and its ability to defend itself and bomb accurately fell well short of what was required. The introduction of the Norden bombsight improved matters and by 1942 a new, improved version of the bomber — the B-17G — began to inflict serious damage on Germany's production facilities. The B-17's huge payload and vast range made it a potent weapon in the lead up to D-Day.

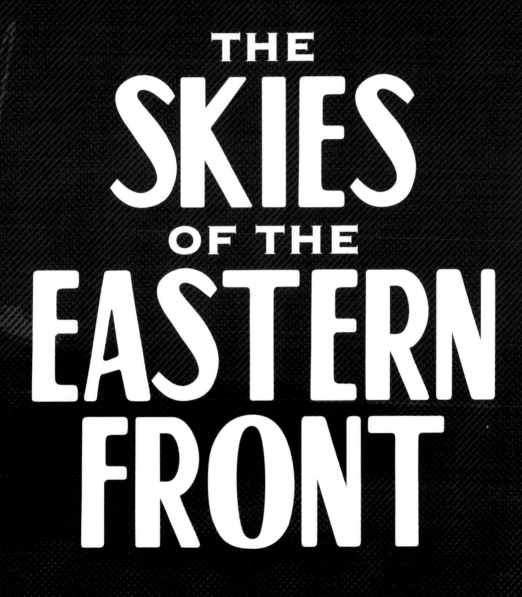

THE
SKIES
OF THE
EASTERN
FRONT

THE WINTER WAR

DATELINE ... 30 NOVEMBER 1939 ... 13 MARCH 1940

Two months after the start of World War II, in November 1939, the Soviet Union invaded Finland. The Red Army's generals had advised Joseph Stalin, the Soviet leader, that the campaign could be concluded in just two weeks. Though the Finns had long anticipated an invasion, they simply did not have the resources to mount an adequate response to the assault. However, 'The Winter War', as it later became known, lasted until March 1940, and the three months of fighting saw serious losses inflicted on the Soviet forces. Remarkably, despite a staggering numerical advantage in terms of planes, the Soviets failed to gain total air superiority, and the *Ilmavoimat* (Finnish Air Force) emerged from the battle stronger than it started.

Molotov Bread Baskets

Finland posed a major problem for the *Voyenno-Vozdushnye Sily* (*VVS*, the Soviet Air Force). With few major industrial cities, strategic targets for Soviet bombers were limited. In addition, the Finnish army fought a highly effective guerrilla campaign, which meant that there were no major troop columns to attack and destroy. Helsinki was hit with 350 bombs, including 'Molotov Bread Baskets', which were an early type of cluster bomb, but minimal damage was caused. There were few roads or bridges to

strike, and the Finnish Army were expert skiers so could easily move directly across the country. Finland's railways were repeatedly bombed, but the tracks were relatively simple to repair and little disruption to troop or supply movements occurred.

In the air, the Soviets initially flew their bombers unescorted by fighters, which made them easy targets for the Finnish Air Force to intercept. Many were shot down or harassed into dropping their bombs early. The Soviet Air Force generals were reluctant to change tactics for fear of displeasing Stalin. General Yakov Alksnis, the previous Air Force Commander, was one of several high profile casualties in the Stalin's infamous purge of disloyal generals in 1938. The new generation of considerably less experienced generals had learnt to keep their heads down and stick to rigid, orthodox military tactics.

The tiny Finnish Air Force of just 100 or so combat-ready aircraft managed to evade complete destruction by the *VVS* air fleet with several thousand planes at its disposal with around 2,000 deployed over Finland. But perhaps the most important factor of all was the training and tactics of the Finnish pilots, who demonstrated the truth of their motto *Qualitas Potentia Nostra* (Quality is Our Strength).

The international trend in the early 1930s was to use a tight, three-plane formation, or 'vic', as a basic fighter element. The fighter pilots in Finland knew that they would never get large numbers of fighters, and they considered the large tight formations ineffective. From studies conducted between 1934 and 1935, the Ilmavoimat developed a loose two-plane section as the basic fighter element. Divisions (four fighters) and flights (eight aircraft) were made of loose sections, but always maintaining the independence of the section. The distance between the fighters in the section was 150 – 200 meters, and the distance between sections in a division was 300 – 400 meters. The principle was always to attack, regardless of numbers; that way the larger enemy formation was broken up and combat became a sequence of section duels, in which the better pilots always won. Finnish fighter training heavily emphasized the complete handling of the fighter and shooting accuracy. Even basic training at the Air Force Academy included a lot of aerobatics with all the basic combat maneuvers and aerial gunnery.

Chief Warrant Officer Ilmari Juutilainen
Fighter Pilot, Ilmavoimat

Demoralizing the *VVS*

The Soviets only changed tactics late in the war, in the face of catastrophic losses – over 200 of their planes were shot down against the loss of just 26 Finnish aircraft (such figures are always difficult to pinpoint accurately in the fog of war, and some post-war estimates put Soviet losses as high as 1,000 aircraft). By the time the *VVS* deployed fighter cover for their bombers, and altered their tactics to deal with the Finnish 'dive attacks', new aircraft had arrived in Finland to help them continue the fight. The Finnish pilots themselves were also by now highly experienced, and could coolly pick off the nervous and increasingly demoralized *VVS* pilots.

When I was close to Antrea, I got a message of three enemy bombers approaching. After about half a minute, I saw three Ilyushin DB-3s approaching. I was about 1,500 feet above them and started the attack turn just like in gunnery camp at Käkisalmi. The DB-3s immediately dropped their bomb loads in the forest and turned back. I shot the three rear gunners, one by one. Then I started to shoot the engines. I followed

(Left) Preparing for take-off inside a Soviet Tupolev SB night bomber.

ILMARI JUUTILAINEN

Born 21 February 1914, Juutilainen was the greatest flying ace of the Finnish Air Force. He claimed 94 confirmed combat victories against Soviet aircraft during the course of World War II, and quite a few more that were unconfirmed. During the Winter War he flew a Fokker D.XXI and scored his first victory on 19 December 1939. He went on to fly a Brewster Buffalo fighter and later in 1943 a Messerschmitt Bf 109 in which he scored 58 of his victories. He always refused an officer's commission in case it prevented him from flying combat missions. He survived the war and died in 1999 at home in Finland on his 85th birthday.

them a long way and kept on shooting. One of them nosed over and crashed. The two others were holed like cheese graters but continued in a shallow, smoking descent. I had spent all of my ammunition, so I turned back. There was no special feeling of real combat. Everything went exactly like training.

Ilmari Juutilainen, recalling one of his many combat encounters with Soviet aircraft

Moscow Peace Treaty

Despite their successes, the Finnish forces were running increasingly short of supplies by March 1940. For their part, the Soviets were increasingly alarmed at the prospect of a protracted and bloody war, and were anxious not to overcommit forces that might soon be sorely needed in battle against the unpredictable German Führer and his *Wehrmacht*. It was in the interests of both sides to draw the conflict to a close, and the Moscow Peace Treaty was signed on 13 March 1940, leaving Finland an independent country in return for 11% of her territory.

Given the overwhelming disparity in the manpower and military hardware between the two combatants, the Winter War was widely seen as a victory for the courageous Finns. More significantly in terms of the overall war, it was seen as a defeat for the Soviet Union. Despite its vast army and air force, the Red Army appeared to be a disorganized and ineffective fighting force. If the Soviet Union could not even conquer Finland, how could she resist the power of the Nazi war machine? The reasoning behind one of Hitler's most catastrophic military blunders, the invasion of the Soviet Union, may well have been initiated by a handful of courageous Finnish pilots in 1939.

(Right) Remains of a Soviet bomber shot down over Helsinki, 1939

YAKOVLEV YAK-1

Small, light, robust and easy to maintain, the Yak-1 was a formidable defensive fighter and no plane played a more significant role in preventing the Luftwaffe gaining air superiority over the skies of Eastern Europe. Its later successors, the Yak-7, Yak-9 and Yak-3 were all, essentially, improvements upon the same basic design, and if considered a single plane the Yak series of aircraft would take the title of the most produced fighter of WWII. In total 37,000 were built — and such staggering production numbers were essential in order to compensate for the enormous losses suffered by the Soviet Union during the war. Between 1941 and 1945 the *VVS* lost 3,336 Yak-1s.

Although a lack of agility made dogfights against German Messerschmitts Bf 109s difficult, the Yak-1's high top speed and excellent visibility counted in its favour. The single 12.7mm UBS machine gun was accurate and reliable enough to give Soviet pilots a fighting chance to inflict serious damage on enemy aircraft, as was demonstrated by the numerous Soviet Aces who scored their kills in Yak planes. Mikhail Baranov shot down four Bf 109s and one Ju 87 in a single day, showing what the Yak-1 could do in the hands of an experienced pilot. Perhaps most importantly, the Yak-1 was relatively simple to build and easy to fly, which meant the Soviet Union could get large numbers of fighter pilots into the sky to counter Luftwaffe attacks. When one of the main factories producing the Yak-1 was bombed on 23 June 1943, production resumed in the smoking ruins just six days later.

Soviet designers had also created the MiG-3 and Il-2, which could at least compete with the Luftwaffe's Bf 109s, FW 190s and Stukas. The MiG-3, with a top speed of 370mph, could match the Bf 109, and while the others were outclassed by their German counterparts, they were nonetheless capable aircraft and available in significant numbers — it is thought that the *VVS* was, at the time, the largest air force in the world.

OPERATION BARBAROSSA

DATELINE ... 22 JUNE 1941 ... 5 DECEMBER 1941

Named after the medieval German ruler Frederick Barbarossa (Red Beard) who, according to legend, would return to rescue Germany in her time of need, Operation Barbarossa was the Nazi campaign to invade and conquer the Soviet Union. The German assault force of 4.5 million troops, supported by 600,000 vehicles, was the largest invasion force in history.

Operation Barbarossa

The non-aggression pact between Germany and Russia signed in 1939, was shattered by the Nazi invasion which appeared to take the Soviet Union by surprise, despite repeated warnings of a huge build-up of German forces. The British had by now broken the encryption codes of the German Enigma machine and passed on information about the forthcoming attack.

The new head of the Soviet government, Joseph Stalin had proclaimed himself Chairman of the Council of People's Commissars on 6 May 1941. He was suspicious of British intentions and remained unconvinced that Adolf Hitler would launch any invasion for at least another year. The German Führer, however, was driven by a desperate desire to defeat the Soviet Union and decided to launch a massive attack before Stalin was fully prepared for war.

The Nazi regime firmly believed that it could secure a quick victory over Stalin's army and air force. Doing so would relieve the growing pressure on German industry and secure the Third Reich's position as the dominant power in mainland Europe. With the Soviet threat eliminated and its valuable resources available to the Nazi war effort, Hitler still believed that Britain would rapidly negotiate peace terms with Germany.

England's hope is Russia and America. If Russia is lost, America will be also, because the loss of Russia will result in an enormous rise of Japan in East Asia. If Russia is smashed, then England's last hope is extinguished. Then Germany will be the master of all Europe and the Balkans.

Führer Adolf Hitler
Address to Senior Nazi Leaders, 1941

An Antiquated Air Force in Decline

On the face of it, Hitler's confidence in a swift and decisive campaign against the Soviets was not unreasonable. The Winter War with Finland had exposed the serious shortcomings of the Red Army and its elderly Air Force, the *Voyenno-Vozdushnye Sily* (*VVS*). The *Wehrmacht* (the unified armed forces of Germany) had enjoyed stunning victories elsewhere in mainland Europe. The only notable defeat for Hitler had come in the Battle of Britain, a battle fought solely in the air. During Operation Barbarossa, Germany could combine air and ground assaults to 'blitzkrieg' their way across Russia, and it was imagined that air superiority could be won easily. The *VVS*, it was believed, was nowhere near as formidable a foe as the British RAF.

HERO OF THE SOVIET UNION

ALEKSANDR POKRYSHKIN

A long-term admirer of the French WWI Ace René Fonck, Aleksandr 'Sasha' Pokryshkin approached flying fighter planes as a science rather than an art. He methodically studied Fonck's memoirs and spent much time attempting to establish the perfect line of attack for a fighter pilot to use. His refusal to follow outdated Soviet orthodoxy when flying resulted in him being grounded and threatened with a court martial. However his detailed research paid off in combat: Pokryshkin flew 550 sorties during the war, participated in 139 aerial engagements with enemy aircraft and shot down 59 planes. Some historians believe the true figure to be even higher, which would make Pokryshkin the most successful fighter pilot on the Allied side. By the end of the war his tactics were being disseminated to all Soviet pilots, and had become the new orthodoxy of the Soviet air force.

However, Pokryshkin's war began in ignominious fashion, as on his very first combat mission he accidentally shot down one of his own bombers. The surprise German invasion of the Soviet Union caused panic and confusion, and against this backdrop Pokryshkin later explained what happened, and how he risked his own life to save the rest of the Soviet bombers.

Pokryshkin felt such a close affinity to his P-39 fighter that he refused to fly any other plane, even when the supposedly superior La-7 fighters became available to him. He made many modifications to the standard aircraft design, including changing the function of the all-important fire button so that it operated his plane's cannons and machine guns at the same time. Pokryshkin received the Hero Of The Soviet Union award three times, along with four Orders of Lenin, four Orders of the Red Banner, two Orders of Suvorov, two Orders of the Red Star and the Order of the October Revolution, making him one of the most decorated Soviet heroes of all time. Pokryshkin survived the war and died in 1985, aged 72.

(Left) Aleksandr Pokryshkin; (right) statue in tribute to Aleksandr Pokryshkin in his home city of Novosibirsk, Russia.

THE SKIES OF THE EASTERN FRONT

In June 1941, the *VVS*, in common with all other Soviet forces, was in a state of flux. Stalin had realized that the opening of hostilities between Germany and the Allies might draw the Soviet Union into a war it was ill-prepared for. He ordered the modernization and expansion of his forces, and over 17,000 military aircraft were produced between 1939 and 1941. But, major problems still beset the *VVS* and the rest of the Russian armed forces.

Stalin's 'purge' of what he considered disloyal generals had resulted in men of limited experience occupying key posts. The planes that were being produced were largely outdated, and many were more or less obsolete by the time they left the factories.

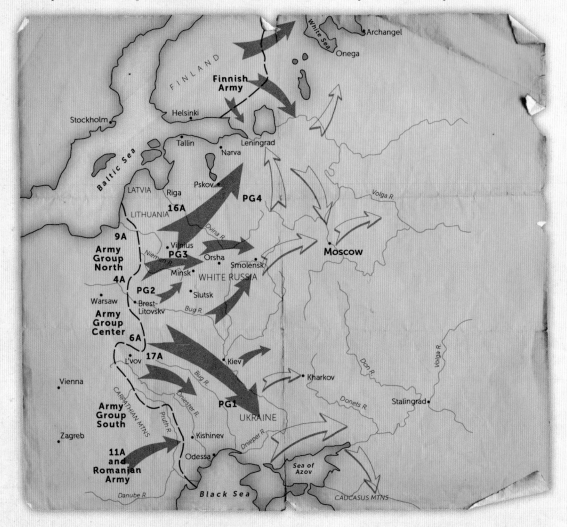

Map showing Operation Barbarossa, the German advance into Russia, 1941.
The distance between the mouth of the River Dvina (or Daugava) near the Latvian capital of Riga on the Baltic Sea in the north and the River Dnieper in the south, draining into the Black Sea, near the Ukrainian seaport of Odessa in the south is around 950 miles (1,500 km). With such an ambitiously long invasion front, it is little wonder that not only the resources of the defending Red Army but also the supply lines of the advancing forces of the Third Reich were stretched to breaking point.

Only squadron commanders' planes were fitted with radios and even these were of poor quality. The Winter War had shown how rigid and old-fashioned tactics were ineffective against modern fighting forces, yet it was difficult to correct these tactics as many were originally endorsed by Stalin himself.

The Ultimate Test of Bravery

Soviet pilots, defending their homeland against a relentlessly driven Nazi war machine intent on committing mass murder, were highly motivated and for the most part well-trained. They were, however, as shocked as Joseph Stalin when Panzers of the Third Reich suddenly rolled across the German Eastern Front on 22 June 1941 and Stukas dive-bombed Soviet air bases, destroying many planes on the ground. It took at least four hours before the order to counter-attack arrived. As they took off in chaotic dribs and drabs, the airmen of the *VVS* knew they were about to face the ultimate test of their skill and bravery.

Germany once again had depended on their infallible triple-action strategy of speed, surprise and overwhelming force to strike decisively against the enemy. The invasion began simultaneously on three separate fronts, with armoured divisions closely supported by dive bombers and fighters. Massive German bombing raids sought to take out as many as possible of the *VVS* aircraft while they remained parked on the ground.

The first days of the battle were an unmitigated disaster for the *VVS*, and Joseph Stalin's propaganda that 'the enemy's finest air units have already been shattered', had a hollow ring to it. It is thought the *VVS* lost over 2,000 planes in the first 18 hours of the campaign, the vast majority of which were destroyed before they even got off the ground. The Luftwaffe, by contrast, reported losses of just 35 aircraft.

Key to the Luftwaffe's success was the use of 'fragmentation bombs' against Soviet airfields. These were delivered with lightning speed by small advance parties of bombers causing widespread partial damage. The idea was to disable large numbers of planes rather than totally destroy just a few, so that the Soviet aircrews could not disperse their assets ahead of the main bombing attack. When the He 111s, Ju 87s and Ju 88s attacked soon afterwards, they targeted the most modern aircraft first. A total of 868 combat aircraft took part in the raids on the first day. Caught off-guard by one of the most devastating surprise aerial attacks the world had ever seen, the Soviet ground response was slow and awkward.

Hitler's initial blitzkrieg into Soviet territory made astonishing progress. By 3 July 1941, German forces had penetrated up to 285 miles (450 km) across the Soviet border, with even the slowest-moving Army Group having conquered 120 miles (190 km).

On the whole, one can say already now that the mission of smashing the mass of the Soviet Army forward of the Dvina and Dnieper has been carried out. It is very likely not saying too much when I observe that the campaign against the Soviet Union has been won in less than fourteen days.

Generaloberst Franz Halder
Chief of German OKH General Staff, Army
3 July 1941

Scorched Earth and an American Pledge

The German premature celebration may have underestimated the sheer manpower available to Stalin. On 22 June 1941, the Soviet Leader issued an order that called-up all available reservists aged from 23 to 37, with the effect that by 1 July 1941, 5.3 million men had been mobilized. The reserve units were hurriedly thrown forward to block any further German progress. Stalin broadcast his first message to his people since the invasion began, calling on farmers to move eastwards away from the German advance, and to destroy anything that might be of use to the enemy.

Faced with such a 'scorched earth' policy the German commanders knew that securing their supply lines was a vital prerequisite before pushing on any further. Although the Luftwaffe had smashed the Soviet Forces in the air, on the ground the scale of the task ahead began to become clear. The first snow began to fall in early October, with the German armies still a long way from Moscow. The dream of a swift victory before the vicious Russian winter descended began to fade. Instead, the German army encircled Leningrad and resolved to starve it into submission rather than risk an all-out assault.

Crucially, with no long range bombers available, the Soviet aircraft production facilities were out of range of the Luftwaffe. The stunning success of the first days of the campaign would ultimately count for nothing as the thousands of destroyed aircraft were steadily replaced. The Luftwaffe had given Germany air superiority, just as Operation Barbarossa required. But Barbarossa presupposed a swift German victory, and events on the ground demonstrated to the German High Command that even when the skies have been conquered, overall victory is far from assured.

The United States had pledged a trillion dollar loan to Stalin, and Britain had already begun to send aircraft and raw materials to the Soviets. It would be a savage winter for both the Germans and the Soviets, but the fact that the Blitzkrieg of Barbarossa was halted before it reached Moscow would prove to be one of the key turning points of the war.

In launching their attack on our country the German fascist invaders calculated that they would be able to 'finish off the Soviet Union for certain in one and a half or two months', and in this short period would succeed in reaching the Urals. It must be said that the Germans did not conceal this plan for a 'lightning' victory. On the contrary, they gave it the utmost publicity. The facts, however, have revealed the utter folly and groundlessness of this 'lightning' plan. Today this crazy plan must be regarded as having definitely failed … Modern war is a war of engines. The war will be won by the side that has an overwhelming preponderance in the output of engines. The combined engine output of the USA, Great Britain and the USSR is at least three times as large as that of Germany. That is one of the grounds for the inevitable doom of Hitler's robber imperialism.

Joseph Stalin
Chairman of the Council of People's Commissars
Address to the Soviet People, 6 November 1941

Berlin Bombing Raids

Despite the vast numerical and technical superiority of their opponents, the *VVS* fought with extraordinary bravery. Many of its pilots would go on to earn the highest

Soviet honour, Hero of the Soviet Union. One of these heroes was Boris Feoktistovich Safonov, who flew his antiquated Polikarpov I-16 fighter into the swarm of Bf 109 and Ju-87s that were attacking the Soviet Union in the summer of 1941. Adorned with the words *Za Stalina!* (For Stalin!) and *Smert Fashistam!* (Death to Fascists!), Safonov completed 109 combat sorties downing 17 of the Luftwaffe's formidable aircraft. In August 1941 alone he accounted for five planes in five days, and the squadron he commanded had accounted for 50 by the time he was declared a Hero of the Soviet Union in September 1941.

Soviet losses throughout the summer were horrendous – and yet Stalin was determined to strike a blow back at his enemy. Göring had declared that the Soviet Air Force was so diminished by Operation Barbarossa that

it posed no threat to the German Fatherland. In response, Stalin sent bombers on an audacious air-raid against Berlin.

The Estonian island of Saaremaa, about 540 miles (870 km) from Berlin was the closest departure point for the *VVS*. During the first bombing raid on 7 August 1941, five Soviet bombers managed to strike Berlin, with a further ten dropping bombs on the reserve target of the port of Szczecin in present day Poland after heavy thunderstorms made reaching Berlin impossible. Other raids followed. None was of huge military significance, but they were crucial in boosting the morale of the *VVS* and the entire Soviet Nation. They also clearly demonstrated to the Nazi leaders that the Soviet Union was far from finished as a fighting force.

Colonel Y. Preobrazhensky (left) and navigator P. Khokhlov at Kagul airfield on the island of Saaremaa, prior to the first bombing attack on Berlin, 7 August 1941.

THE BATTLE OF STALINGRAD

In the late summer of 1942, Luftwaffe bombers reduced much of the south-western Russian city of Stalingrad (present-day Volgograd) to rubble in a series of devastating attacks. Over a thousand tons of bombs were dropped on the city and its crucial supply line, the Volga waterway. Almost 1,000 people were killed and 41 Soviet ships were sunk or badly damaged. The Russian Air Force (*VVS*) suffered appalling losses during combat engagements with the Luftwaffe when over 200 aircraft were destroyed in a single week during August 1942.

The Battle of Stalingrad

Although the Soviet Air Force's brave pilots continued to throw themselves into the battle, Germany ruled the skies in 1942 and could destroy any target they were asked to. General Friedrich Paulus, who had been ordered by Hitler to take the city, then moved his 6th Army and the 4th Panzers in to mop up any remaining resistance in Stalingrad. The Germans had already conquered almost a million square miles of Soviet territory, and suspected that the Red Army was despondent and close to collapse. Events in the following months would show that nothing could be further from the truth.

The Soviets resisted ferociously, fighting from street to street and house to house. In such circumstances there was little the Luftwaffe could do to help and their threat was diminished. Indeed the Red Army's tactic was to keep the fighting at close quarters, 'hugging the enemy' in order to mitigate the threat from the air and from the German Panzers. Progress for the German invaders was agonizingly slow and murderously difficult. Stalingrad was being defended to the death by the 62nd and 64th Russian Armies under the command of General Vasily Chuikov. A battle-hardened soldier known as 'The Man of Iron Will' and veteran of the 1939 invasion of Poland and the 1940 Russo-Finnish war, Chuikov was not a man to give way easily.

The Germans underestimated our artillery. And they underestimated the effectiveness of our infantry against their tanks. This battle showed that tanks forced to operate in narrow quarters are of limited value; they're just guns without mobility. In such conditions nothing can take the place of small groups of infantry, properly armed, and fighting with utmost determination. I don't mean barricade street fighting – there was little of that – but groups converting every building into a fortress and fighting for it floor by floor and even room by room. Such defenders cannot be driven out either by tanks or planes. The Germans dropped over a million bombs on us but they did not dislodge our infantry from its decisive positions. On the other hand, tanks can be destroyed from buildings used as fortresses.

General Vasily Chuikov, Commander 62nd Army
Battle of Stalingrad

The Russians not only have held defensively but have unleashed attack after attack ... In three days we advanced 1300 yards. Yesterday and today we were only able to turn in our holes in the earth. As Columbus first saw land, so we look toward Stalingrad, of which we are talking as one talks of the moon ... First we take five houses and then must give up two ... The soldiers talk of what they would do if Stalingrad were behind them. Already it is growing cold.

Anonymous German officer as reported in Deutsche Allgemeine Zeitung newspaper

We have fought during 15 days for a single house, with mortars, grenades, machine guns, and bayonets. Already by the third day 54 German corpses are strewn in the cellars, on the landings, and the staircases. The front is a corridor between burnt-out rooms; it is the thin ceiling between two floors. Help comes from neighboring houses by fire escapes and chimneys. There is a ceaseless struggle from noon to night ... faces black with

"The street is no longer measured by meters ... but by corpses ..."

sweat, we bombard each other with grenades in the middle of explosions, clouds of dust and smoke, heaps of mortar, floods of blood, fragments of furniture and human beings. Ask any soldier what half an hour of hand-to-hand struggle means in such a fight. And imagine Stalingrad; 80 days and 80 nights of hand-to-hand struggles. The street is no longer measured by meters ... but by corpses ... Stalingrad is no longer a town. By day it is an enormous cloud of burning, blinding smoke; it is a vast furnace lit by the reflection of the flames. And when night arrives, one of those scorching, howling, bleeding nights, the dogs plunge into the Volga and swim desperately to gain the other bank. The nights of Stalingrad are a terror for them. Animals flee this hell; the hardest stones can not bear it for long; only men endure.

Anonymous German soldier, Stalingrad 1942
An evocative description of the fighting

A squadron of German Stukas flies towards Stalingrad, September 1942.

IVAN KOZHEDUB

A true legend of what the Soviets called 'The Great Patriotic War', Ukrainian born Ivan Mykytovych Kozhedub was also the highest-scoring Ace on the Allied side of World War II. For his astonishing tally of 62 kills over 326 combat missions, Kozhedub was three times awarded the highest Soviet Award of 'Hero of the Soviet Union'.

Kozhedub spoke after the war of his close personal connection with his aircraft. It was purchased for him by Vasily Koniyev, a beekeeper from a Bolshevik collective farm. Koniyev asked that Kozhedub name the plane after the nephew of the famous Marshal Vasily Konev, who was killed at the start of the war. Kozhedub's donated plane did indeed prove to have a sting in the tail … he downed eight German aircraft with it, including five Fw 190s.

After the war Kozhedub stayed in the military and was later promoted to General. He died in Moscow in August 1991.

Red Storm Rising

When the Germans finally succeeded in pushing the Soviets back to the west bank of the Volga, the Luftwaffe again rained bombs down upon the Red Army positions, flying up to 2,000 sorties a day in October. The Soviets were forced into an ever-shrinking pocket which soon stretched for just 1,000 yards (910 m). Over 1,200 Stuka sorties were flown to decimate the remaining troops. Although Soviet losses continued to mount at a horrific rate, reinforcements also continued to pour in, and General Paulus could not break the last lines of resistance.

But the constant raids were beginning to take their toll on the Luftwaffe, too. By November, almost half of its original strength of 1,600 aircraft had been lost or were no longer serviceable after the 20,000 sorties flown. The planes — and pilots — were difficult to replace. The Soviets, who had relocated their key manufacturing sites further east, were increasing their own production rates all the time. In 1942 they turned out almost 23,000 new combat aircraft, as opposed to Germany's 15,000.

The Soviet planes produced were getting better and better, too. The Ilyushin Il-2, which accounted for around a third of all planes produced, was proving to be a dive-bomber capable of causing serious losses to German panzer divisions. As more Luftwaffe planes were required to combat the Allied landings in North Africa, increasingly the German Air Force found itself being stretched to breaking point on the Eastern Front. The balance of power between the two sides was shifting … and it was about to shift even more decisively.

Operation Uranus and the Stalingrad Airdrops

The German 6th Army's northern and southern flanks were protected by Italian, Hungarian and Romanian units. The Soviet generals Zhukov and Vasilevsky believed these flanks were vulnerable as the units had inferior equipment, morale and experience compared to the rest of the German Army. Operation Uranus, launched on 19 November 1942 by the Red Army, was an ambitious attempt to exploit this weakness and encircle the invaders.

Just as the Soviets had anticipated, the weaker units defending the flanks collapsed when faced with a massive Red Army counter-attack. Two days later, the Soviet forces pushing south met those pushing north near the town of Kalach, 250 miles (400 km) north of Stalingrad. Almost 300,000 Axis troops, most of them German, now found themselves surrounded on all sides; trapped in the ruins of Stalingrad. With no way to resupply the beleaguered troops by land or sea, the only option was to airdrop supplies.

Reichsmarschall Hermann Göring, the Luftwaffe Commander-in-Chief, was confident as ever, that his Air Force was up to the job. A similar operation had relieved German troops encircled near Leningrad earlier in the campaign. But in Leningrad only a single army division had been trapped. In Stalingrad, the Luftwaffe were faced with supplying an entire isolated and besieged army.

Operation Winter Storm

Generalfeldmarschall of the Luftwaffe, Wolfram von Richthofen, immediately highlighted the madness of the scheme, and was backed up by one of the most prominent commanders of the *Wehrmacht, Feldmarschall* Erich von Manstein of Army Group Don, who had been ordered to launch a relief effort to rescue General Friedrich Paulus and the 6th Army. von Manstein's troops got within 35 miles (56 km) of Stalingrad during 'Operation Winter Storm' but could not break through to relieve his comrades. Instead he urged Hitler to order Paulus to break out, which would surrender the city to the Soviets but spare the lives of Paulus' troops. Hitler insisted that Paulus hold the city or die in the attempt.

The trapped Axis forces suffered horribly throughout the frozen winter of 1942. The Luftwaffe stretched itself to breaking point trying to achieve the impossible and drop adequate supplies to them. But the maximum they could deliver with the planes available was around 117 tons a day, and the army needed closer to 800 tons a day.

Soviet anti-aircraft fire was ferocious, and more and more *VVS* fighters patrolled the approaches to Stalingrad. Atrocious weather conditions made flying treacherous even when the German planes could evade enemy attack. Soviet forces then assaulted the airfields that the Luftwaffe flew from, forcing them to retreat to Salsk, almost 200 miles (320 km) from Stalingrad.

Longer journey times meant greater exposure to enemy fighters, with inevitable results. In total, 488 German aircraft were lost. Many more were destroyed both on the ground and in the air in the coming months, and the airdrops petered out as the German troops starved to death in Stalingrad.

A Noble Surrender

Eventually General Paulus requested permission to surrender. Hitler responded by promoting him to *Generalfeldmarschall*. The message to Paulus was clear. No German *Generalfeldmarschall* had ever been taken prisoner: he should commit suicide or fight on to the death rather than suffer the ignoble fate of capture. Paulus, however, wanted to spare his own life and those of his remaining 91,000 men, and much to Hitler's dismay he surrendered on 2 February 1943. In the end, very few of Paulus' men would be saved. It is estimated that only 5,000 of the 91,000 taken prisoner at Stalingrad made it home alive. The rest became victims of the Soviet labour camps. They joined a long list of victims of the Battle of Stalingrad.

Friedrich Paulus, on the other hand, did survive his incarceration and became a vocal critic of the Nazi regime, later acting as a witness at the Nuremberg War trials of the Nazi leaders. In return for his cooperation, he was allowed to be released in 1953, two years ahead of most of the remaining German POWs. Paulus lived and worked for three years in Dresden, East Germany until his

death in 1957, 14 years after the surrender in Stalingrad.

The Axis forces lost between 500,000 and 850,000 men, and the Soviet Army well over a million men. It was one of the bloodiest battles of the entire war, and cost both sides heavily in men and machinery. The Soviets, however, were turning out new planes and tanks at a prodigious rate, and had a vast army to call upon. Germany, on the other hand, was badly weakened and struggled to replace either the experienced troops or the planes and tanks lost.

The defeat of Stalingrad was a momentous blow to Hitler. The battle had lasted five months, one week and three days. His planned invasion of the Soviet Union was failing badly. Elsewhere the once invincible German armed forces were facing resistance and reversals. The *Wehrmacht* never regained the initiative on the Eastern Front and had redeployed vast numbers of men from western Europe to reinforce a doomed campaign, many of whom were never seen by their families again.

A crashed German Bf 109 in the ruins of Stalingrad.

FEMALE SOVIET PILOTS

Marina Raskova

When Hitler invaded Russia, Joseph Stalin had called for anyone strong enough to pick up a rifle to join the Soviet Armed Forces to fight in WWII. Almost a million women volunteered, many of whom were utilized in front-line combat missions. In the air, combat aviation units began to be formed in October 1941, largely as a result of a Russian female navigator, Marina Raskova, using her personal influence with Joseph Stalin to persuade him of the potential of female fighter pilots.

Marina Raskova was commander of the 125th Guards Bomber Aviation Regiment until she and the entire crew of her Petlyakov Pe-2 were killed in 1943 whilst making a forced landing on the banks of the Volga near Stalingrad.

The Night Witches

Many women were engaged in the bitter air war that caused massive loss of life on both sides. The 46th Taman Guards Night Bomber Aviation regiment was the best known of the Russian female air regiments and remained solely female throughout the war. The women flew antiquated Polikarpov Po-2 biplanes which were no match for the Luftwaffe's modern aircraft and were easily set on fire. Flying an ancient Russian Po-2 and being caught by a German Bf 109 fighter usually meant certain death for the Soviet pilots, since parachutes were not provided to them until late in 1944. But the women's night bombing raids caused much damage and consternation to the German forces who respectfully named them *die Nachthexen* (The Night Witches).

Lydia Litvyak

One of the most celebrated female pilots was Lydia 'Lilya' Litvyak 'The White Rose of Stalingrad', who flew 168 missions in her Yak-1 aircraft and accounted for 12 German aircraft with three further shared victories. She was the world's first female fighter pilot to earn the title 'ace'. She was shot down and killed on 1 August 1943 whilst flying her third sortie of the day during the Battle of Kursk. By that time her fame had become an embarrassment to the Luftwaffe and eight Messerschmitt Bf 109s made a coordinated attack upon her to ensure she would not live to see her 23rd birthday. Her remains were eventually discovered in 1979 near the village of Dmitriyevka, about 70 miles (110 km) north west of Kursk and were recovered for an official burial. In 1990 she was posthumously awarded the title of Hero of the Soviet Union.

(Left) Marina Raskova; (right) Lydia Litvyak.

THE BATTLE OF KURSK

DATELINE ... 5 JULY 1943 ... 23 AUGUST 1943

Though vast armies of tanks fought an epic battle on the ground, the outcome would largely be decided in the skies above them. The Battle of Kursk was the largest aerial battle of the entire war, and also saw the costliest single day of aerial warfare in history. Each side committed vast numbers of aircraft, knowing that air superiority for either side would result in certain victory. In total it is estimated that over 4,000 aircraft took part in the battle.

The Battle of Kursk

By the summer of 1943, Axis forces had occupied Soviet territory for two years, but were making little progress in their march to Moscow. Hitler could not afford to be drawn into a costly war of attrition

now that the Allies were attacking the German homeland from the West. Göring's Luftwaffe had been suffering terrible losses, and it was clear they were now being stretched too thinly. As a result, Operation Citadel, a massive combined attack, was planned on Soviet positions at Kursk, in south-west Russia, near the border with present-day Ukraine, in the hope that air superiority could be established and a large portion of the Red Army surrounded and then destroyed.

A succession of delays meant that the date of the German push was put back several times. This gave the Soviets more time to dig in and prepare defensive positions for the attack that they had already been warned by British Intelligence was about to come. Soviet factories were by now turning out more modern planes such as the La-5F and Yak-9 at a prodigious rate. Nonetheless, the *VVS* had continued to suffer severe losses in encounters with the Luftwaffe. In general, Soviet pilots switched away from engaging with German fighters and concentrated on simply defending their own bombers in order to keep losses at an acceptable level. The Luftwaffe, too, was under strain after flying huge numbers of sorties in the east and suffering several defeats at the hands of Allied aircraft in western Europe. The delay to the start of the battle gave both sides a chance to regain their strength, which made the battle itself all the more ferocious when it finally began on 5 July 1943.

Blitzkrieg Tactics

Six thousand tanks are believed to have taken part in the fighting, making Kursk the largest tank battle in history. German Panzers were forced to weave through Soviet minefields and pre-sighted artillery 'kill-zones' where row upon row of anti-tank guns confronted them. The defensive positions erected by the Red Army were ten times deeper than the famous Maginot Line in France. This nullified the lightning fast advances of the spearheading German mechanized divisions which was the primary speed and surprise strategy behind the German blitzkrieg method of warfare. The secondary tactic which was always combined with the motorized ground advance of blitzkrieg, was the swift, devastating deployment of

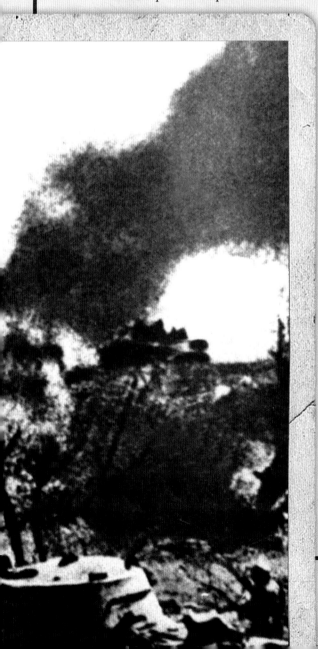

Soviet tanks and aircraft launch an attack at the Battle of Kursk.

ILYUSHIN IL-2

Widely deployed on the Eastern Front, the Ilyushin Il-2 Soviet ground attack aircraft was capable of blowing up the Panther and Tiger tanks of the Nazi Panzer Divisions. They attacked ground positions and the close formations of Luftwaffe transport aircraft and were most successful against the Junkers Ju-52. However while the Il-2 was a deadly air to ground attack weapon they were vulnerable to mid-air battles with the faster Messerschmitt Bf 109s and Focke-Wulf Fw 190s.

Having suffered heavy losses against the German fighters a rear gunner was introduced in 1942 equipped with a 12.7mm UBT machine gun. The semi-turret gun mount allowed the machine gun to be fired at angles of up to 35 degrees upwards. Terrified and under attack, German ground troops gave the Il-2 the nickname *Der Schlächter* (The Slaughterer) or *Der Schwarze Tod* (The Black Death), while to the Il-2 pilots it was simply the *Ilyusha*. When manufacture of the aircraft began to slow down, Joseph Stalin demanded faster production saying that the Il-2 was 'as essential to the Red Army as air and bread'.

heavy air support as 'flying artillery' to force a breakthrough and confuse the enemy by constantly switching the principal point of attack. In order to repel the German aerial assault, the *VVS* would have to counter the Luftwaffe in much the same way as the Red Army was thwarting the Panzer divisions on the ground.

Consequently, in an attempt to relief the escalating blitzkrieg pressure, the Soviets launched a daring counter-attack on the morning of 5 July 1943, aimed at destroying the Luftwaffe's air assets on the ground. A total of 132 Ilyushin Il-2s ground attack aircraft supported by 285 fighters approached the airfields at Belgorod, Kharkov, Poltava and Dnepropetrovsk. However, early detection by German radar wrecked the surprise attack and the Soviet aircraft were met by swarms of Bf 109s. Even the *VVS's* improved fighters could not handle such large numbers of Messerschmitts, flown by highly experienced Luftwaffe pilots. The operation proved to be a disaster, with relatively little damage caused and 120 Soviet planes shot down.

Combined Ground and Air Attack

The Soviet aerial counter-attack left the Red Army more exposed as the German Panzers forced their way towards Kursk. The German plan called for a classic 'pincer movement' with two separate attacks, one from the north and one from the south combining to encircle the Red Army. Initially, the Germans made good progress on both fronts, albeit with heavy losses. In the north in particular, the *VVS* response was piecemeal and chaotic, and the Ilyushin Il-2s sent to attack the German tanks too often arrived without fighter cover.

They were easily picked off by Luftwaffe Bf 109s and Fw 190s. The shortage of *VVS* fighters gave the Luftwaffe temporary air-superiority and they made it pay.

Ju 87D Stukas were fitted with 37mm anti-tank guns and used as 'tankbusters' rather than straightforward dive-bombers as they had been previously. The Luftwaffe's *Schlactsgeschwaders* (ground attack wings) also used Henschel Hs 129 B-2 aircraft, nicknamed *Panzerknacker* ('tank-cracker') to blast the Soviets with 30mm cannon fire whilst Fw 190s dropped fragmentation bombs.

Heavier bombing raids were carried out by Heinkel He IIIs and Junkers Ju 88s, while Bf 109s provided fighter cover. It was discovered that German 88mm anti-aircraft guns were especially effective when used against tanks, so many were moved from defending airfields to the battlefield itself. The combination of this awesome fire-power, along with the lack of a co-ordinated response from the *VVS* meant that the Germans had made ominous advances by the end of the first day.

The Soviets regrouped, using Ilyushin Il-2 ground-attack planes in larger formations and supporting them with fighters, and the difference it made to the battle on the ground was enormous. German tank losses rose dramatically, and while the Bf 109s continued to have the better of any dogfights with Soviet fighters, they too were losing aircraft far more rapidly than they could replace them. By 12 July 1943, the Germans knew they had to make a decisive breakthrough or the battle would be lost. The Soviets were by then confident enough to countenance a massive counter-attack to throw the Germans off balance. The stage was set for a giant confrontation between the two sides. The ensuing battle was brutal on the ground but even more savage in the air. It became the costliest single day in the history of aerial warfare.

The Battle of Prokhorovka

The advancing German 4th Panzer Army collided with the Soviet 5th Guards Army, heading the opposite way, just west of the town of Prokhorovka, about 60 miles (100 km) south of Kursk. Each side called for air support and waves of Hs 129s and Ju 87s attacked the Soviet positions as Ilyushin Il-2s hammered the Panzers. Hundreds of fighter plane dogfights erupted throughout the day. The German tanks on the ground were heavily outnumbered by the Red Army but, with the help of the Luftwaffe, they managed to inflict catastrophic losses on their less well-organized enemy. However, the German advance was gradually squeezed as the Soviet flanking positions held firm. The narrowness of the passage the Panzers had punched in the Soviet positions soon became problematic and the Germans discovered new defensive lines beyond the ones they had already broken. In the end, although the German forces managed to shatter the planned Soviet offensive, they could not do enough to break the Red Army's deep defensive lines. Severely depleted, the Germans were forced to withdraw.

Blitzkrieg Aborted

Events elsewhere now caused Hitler to change his mind about the entire offensive. On the night of 9/10 July 1943, Allied forces mounted an amphibious assault on Sicily. Despite vigorous protests from *Feldmarschalls* von Kluge and von Manstein, Hitler decided to abandon Operation Citadel. The commanders on the ground were convinced that they had broken the back of Soviet resistance and that given a little more time they could establish total air superiority and rout the Soviet forces. Hitler's decision, however, was final, and it remains to this day one of the most controversial he made in the war.

Perhaps if they had fought on the Germans would indeed have won at Kursk. As it was, their withdrawal was rapidly followed by Soviet counter-offensives which saw them take Belgorod and Orel before finally taking Kharkov, which Hitler had previously sworn to defend at all costs. Before the end of autumn, Soviet troops had crossed the Dnieper and liberated Kiev. The Battle of Kursk was the first example of a major German ground offensive being successfully halted and reversed. A large part of the Soviet success was due to the *VVS* denying the Luftwaffe air superiority, a luxury enjoyed by every prior ground offensive the Germans had embarked upon.

The cost for the Soviets was extra-ordinarily high, however. In addition to the tens of thousands of men killed on the ground, the *VVS* itself lost around 1,000 aircraft in the struggle. Germans losses were lower, though still unsustainably high. But crucially in terms of the overall war, the Battle of Kursk marked a distinct change in the momentum of the war on the Eastern Front. The Soviets, who for so long had been desperately defending themselves against German assaults, were now on the offensive.

The Black Devil of the South

Erich Hartmann

Erich Alfred Hartmann was 'Bubi' ('young boy') to his friends, and 'The Black Devil of the South' to his enemies — the vast majority of whom were Soviet pilots. Hartmann holds the distinguished accolade of being the highest-scoring fighter ace in the history of aerial warfare, with a truly incredible tally of 352 aerial victories. Some 345 of these were against Soviet opposition. He didn't have things all his own way by any means — he was forced to bail out or crash land no fewer than 14 times — but his record throughout WWII was unsurpassed by any other pilot and he is considered to be the 'Ace of Aces' as a result. Unsurprisingly, he was awarded the coveted Knight's Cross of the Iron Cross with Oak Leaves, Swords and Diamonds for his achievements.

Erich Hartmann joined the Luftwaffe in 1940 aged 18, and completed his fighter pilot training in 1942. He was posted to the Eastern Front, but was fortunate enough to join *Jagdgeschwader* 52, where he was coached to fly Messerschmitt Bf 109s by some of the Luftwaffe's most brilliant fighter aces. The young Hartmann did not always cover himself in glory. For indulging his passion for aerobatics in a Bf 109 he was grounded for three months. The grounding actually saved his life — the aircraft he had been scheduled to fly developed problems and crash landed, killing his roommate who had taken Hartmann's place at the controls. Hartmann had yet to learn his lesson, however, and his first combat mission of WWII ended with him crash-landing his aircraft after running out of fuel in his eagerness to chase enemy aircraft in pursuit of his first kill. That kill duly came in November 1942, but by the end of the year he had added only one further kill to his tally.

Things began to change with the Battle of Kursk, during which Hartmann shot down seven Soviet planes in a single day. With his confidence at a new high, he began to score consistently, getting in as close as possible to his enemies to conserve ammunition. He survived being shot down behind enemy lines and managed to return to the front, where his success rate soared against the less experienced and less well-equipped Soviet pilots.

So quickly did he rack up kills, that Luftwaffe High Command had his scores double- and triple-checked for accuracy. By 2 March 1944, his tally had reached 202 kills. The Soviet pilots were so terrified of his deadly prowess that many refused to engage

(Right) Messerschmitt Bf 109.

him in combat when they spotted the 'Black Tulip' design on his plane. Noticing that this was beginning to affect his success rate, Hartmann had the design removed.

In May 1944, Hartmann encountered American fighters for the first time, shooting down two Mustang P-51s in the skies over Bucharest. The more modern US fighters represented a far greater challenge to the German Ace, but nonetheless on 17 August he overtook fellow JG 52 pilot Gerhard Barkhorn's total of 273 kills to become the top scoring fighter ace of the war.

Hartmann broke the 300 mark with a characteristically successful day's combat on 24 August 1944, when he downed 11 planes in two separate combat missions. Luftwaffe High Command ordered him to be grounded for fear of the effect on morale should he be killed, but Hartmann successfully lobbied to be reinstated and continued to fly throughout the rest of the war. His last kill came on 8 May 1945, the last day of the war in Europe, over Brno, Czechoslovakia, when he shot down a Soviet Yak-9. By the time he landed he was told the Red Army was within artillery range of the airfield and so he destroyed his Bf 109. Despite being ordered to fly to the British zone to avoid capture by the Soviets he had so tormented, Hartmann elected to stay. He claimed that this was the only order he ever disobeyed during the war, and stated that if he left his men 'that would have been bad leadership'.

The Soviets charged Hartmann with war crimes related to the murder of civilians. The charge was false but he was found guilty nonetheless and sentenced to 25 years hard labour. After 10 years in the Soviet Gulags, Hartmann was finally released in 1955. He returned to West Germany to become an officer in the West German Air Force, retiring in 1970. He died in 1993, aged 71. Four years after his death, in 1997, the Russian government admitted the war crimes charges against Hartmann had been invented, and formally exonerated him of all guilt.

THE
SKIES
OF THE
MEDITERRANEAN
AND
NORTH AFRICA

THE GERMAN INVASION OF CRETE

DATELINE ... 20 MAY 1941 ... 30 MAY 1941

The German paratroop assault on the Greek island of Crete in the Mediterranean Sea, was a short and extremely bloody affair that held major significance for future deployment of airborne forces during the rest of the war. The assault from the air was the first ever attempt in military history to use *Fallschirmjäger* (paratroops) in a large-scale strategic invasion. The Allies knew that an attack was imminent, from information gleaned after breaking the German Enigma machine codes but were anticipating an amphibious assault. The innovative German airborne tactics threw their plans into disarray and the result was a chaotic battle involving the Armies, Navies and Air Forces of both the Allied and Axis powers.

A Leap into the Unknown

The Nazi plan was to capture key airfields on the island and then use them to land supplies and ground forces once they were secure. Maleme Airfield on Crete's north-western coast was the target of the first paratroopers to leap from the Junkers Ju 52 at around 08:00 hours on the morning of 20 May 1941. The airfield was heavily defended, and the New Zealand troops stationed there under Major-General Bernard Freyberg were expecting trouble. Consequently, German losses were catastrophic. 400 of the airborne battalion's 600 men were dead by the end of the day.

About 12 miles (20 km) to the east, instead of parachuting into the combat zone, gliders carrying infantry units were landing near the town of Chania, where the Greek and New Zealand artillery defenders dealt them an equally savage blow. The glider troops were hit by mortar fire within seconds of landing and were almost totally annihilated.

The first invading forces did not come anywhere close to taking the airfields that had been their primary objectives. A second and third wave of paratroopers and glider-borne troops also met fierce resistance in the afternoon and failed to capture the smaller airfields at the coastal cities of Rethimnon and Heraklion. In total 750 glider-borne troops and 10,000 paratroops were used in the invasion, along with 5,000 airlifted mountain soldiers.

During the night of 20 May 1941, however, the Allied defenders made a critical mistake. The New Zealand infantry battalion defending a key hill above Maleme Airfield was withdrawn, apparently in error, effectively handing the Germans control of the airfield when day broke. The paratroopers set up a highly effective defensive line at Maleme and could not be dislodged. This foothold allowed German reinforcements to pour into Crete from the sea.

The Royal Navy and Royal Air Force fought desperately to stop the new troops from landing, and in ferocious fighting by land, sea and air, serious losses were suffered by both sides. In the end, the Germans overwhelmed the Allied defenders and took control of the island.

Counting the Cost

At least 3,600 Germans were killed and several thousand more wounded. Around

(Right) German aircraft dropping paratroopers during the invasion of Crete, 1941.

a third of the Ju 52s used in the operation were destroyed or damaged.

The Royal Navy lost 2,000 men, six destroyers and three cruisers trying to defend the island, with a further two battleships, seven destroyers and one aircraft carrier damaged. The RAF lost 47 aircraft. Even Hitler was shocked at the casualties involved. He ordered that no more major airborne or glider assaults be launched, and this order remained in effect for the rest of the war.

The Allies took a different lesson from the Battle of Crete, and began urgently to form airborne divisions of their own. These paratroops were to play crucial offensive roles in Allied operations later in the war at Arnhem in Holland, supporting the D-Day invasion in 1944 and the crossing of the Rhine in 1945.

SUNDERLAND FLYING BOAT

The S.25 Sunderland was a British flying boat patrol bomber developed for the Royal Air Force by aircraft manufacturer Short Brothers. It was one of the most impressively armed and widely used flying boats throughout World War II. Originally intended to have a crew of seven this was later increased to eleven, when extra gunners were added to man the Sunderland's escalating array of firepower.

Developed from passenger-carrying civilian flying boats, the militarized version of the Sunderland became indispensable during World War II. It was especially valuable in the evacuation of troops after the German invasion of Crete and the rescue of the stricken crews of Allied shipping after German U-boat attacks in the Atlantic.

As British tactics against the German submarines improved and aircrew gained combat experience, the Sunderland Mark I benefitted from various armament upgrades turning it into a well-armed fighting machine that was difficult to shoot down. With machine guns in the nose and tail as well as a dorsal gun turret, the Sunderland bristled with enough guns for the Germans to give it the nickname *Der Fliegendes Stachelschwein* (The Flying Porcupine).

On 2 June 1943, the Sunderland gained legendary status during an air battle between eight Junkers Ju 88C Luftwaffe fighters and a single Sunderland Mark III of RAF 46 Squadron. The 11 crewmen on board the Sunderland had been searching for survivors of a shot down airliner over the Bay of Biscay when they spotted the eight German fighters. In the fierce fire fight that followed, the Sunderland's nose, dorsal and tail guns all scored spectacular hits, shooting down six of the eight Ju 88Cs. The Sunderland suffered severe damage and one of the gunners was dead, but they made it back to the south coast of England landing at Praa Sands in Cornwall.

THE SIEGE OF MALTA

The tiny island of Malta, about 50 miles (80 km) south of the Italian island of Sicily in the Mediterranean Sea, was of huge strategic importance in World War II. Initially it provided a base for the Royal Navy, allowing British sea power ensure that access to vital resources remained open. Later, when the campaign in North Africa and the Middle East intensified, it provided a base to attack German forces and disrupt Nazi supply lines. Indeed, Field Marshal Erwin Rommel, legendary Commander of the Third Reich's *Afrika Korps* warned of Malta's significance as early as May 1941 when he said, 'Without Malta, the Axis will end by losing control of North Africa.'

Defending the Indefensible

The Italian Navy had been tamed by the British naval and aerial forces in the Mediterranean region, and so the Axis powers resolved to bomb Malta into submission before launching their planned invasion with 'Operation Herkules'. British Chiefs of Staff had suggested at the outbreak of war that Malta was indefensible, but Churchill proposed defending the island with fighter planes delivered by aircraft carriers in 'Club Runs' from Britain. Malta was beyond the range of British fighter planes and so the carriers would move them part of the way then 'fly off' planes that had been fitted with 'ferry tanks' containing the extra fuel required to reach Malta.

The siege lasted from 1940 to 1943, but perhaps the most critical period of the monumental struggle came in 1942, when Spitfires arrived on the island to supplement Hurricanes in taking on the Luftwaffe's bombers and fighters. The new reinforcements had an immediate effect. Canadian Ace George Beurling, later known as the 'Knight of Malta', shot down 27 Axis planes in just 14 days during the spring of 1942.

By August 1942, 163 Spitfires had been successfully delivered to the island, in time to do battle with an increasingly desperate Luftwaffe. Both sides knew that a decisive battle between Rommel and Field Marshal Bernard Montgomery, Commander of the British 8th Army was looming in North Africa, and so, in early October, the German Air Force launched a ferocious new assault on Malta.

Switching to All-Out Attack

For 17 days vast waves of German bombers and fighters were engaged by the island's Spitfires and Hurricanes. The losses were high on both sides. The Luftwaffe lost 34 Ju 88s and 12 Bf 109s, with a further 18 planes damaged. The RAF lost 43 Spitfires, of which 23 were completely destroyed. The British defensive line held – just. The losses it inflicted on the Luftwaffe were just too high. In November 1942, a convoy of four British merchant ships reached Malta from Alexandria, effectively breaking the siege of the island.

From December 1942, the Common-wealth Air Forces on Malta transformed their combat plans from strictly defensive mode to all-out attack and, just as Rommel feared, the result was devastating for Axis supply lines.

By May 1943, air and sea forces operating out of Malta had sunk 230 Axis ships in just 164 days. A rate of destruction unsurpassed in any other battle. The 3,340th German air raid on Malta occurred on 20 July 1943. It was the last inflicted upon the island. A total of 30,000 buildings had been destroyed in the three years of the Axis bombing campaign.

King George VI announced from London: 'To honour her brave people, I award the George Cross to the Island Fortress of Malta, to bear witness to a heroism and a devotion that will long be famous in history.'

Malta was the first British Commonwealth country to receive the bravery award, which is normally only awarded to individuals. To this day, the George Cross is proudly commemorated on the red and white national flag of Malta.

THE MALTESE CROSS AND THE KNIGHTS OF MALTA

The George Cross should not be mistaken for the Maltese Cross. Since Maltese independence in 1964, the George Cross awarded to Malta by King George VI in 1942 is depicted in the top left corner of Malta's red and white flag. However, the Maltese Cross is a much more historic symbol having originated during the Middle Ages. Its eight-pointed design is associated with one of the most famous religious military orders of the Christian crusaders, the Knights Hospitalier. Also known as the Knights of St John, because of their dedication to St John the Baptist, the knights were gifted the island of Malta in 1530 by King Charles V of Spain in exchange for an annual fee of a Maltese Falcon which they were to send him on All Souls Day each year.

After they successfully defended Malta from invasion by the armies of the Ottoman Empire in 1565, in what became known the First Great Siege, the Knights of Malta continued to defend the island for the next 268 years transforming it into a proud prosperous island of trade and enterprise.

Briefly among their order, in 1608, was the Italian artist Caravaggio whose great masterpiece, *The Beheading of St John the Baptist,* was commissioned by the Knights of Malta and can still be seen today hanging in St John's Co-Cathedral in Valetta, Malta. The beautiful cathedral survived the bombs of World War II and is considered to be one the world's great churches. Built by the Knights between 1573 and 1578 with richly decorated, marble in-laid tombstones in the nave of the church, marking the graves of buried dead warrior knights. About 10 minutes walk south, stands the Malta Memorial commemorating warrior heroes fallen in the conflict of a later century — the Commonwealth airmen who lost their lives during World War II and who have no known grave.

The ornate interior of St John's Co-Cathedral, Malta.

THE KNIGHT OF MALTA
GEORGE 'BUZZ' BEURLING

In 1938, Canada's most famous war hero, Buzz Beurling, was a skinny 17-year-old in Montreal, itching to become a fighter pilot. He had visions of joining the Chinese Air Force to help them overcome a Japanese invasion in the Sino-Japanese War, before turning to the Royal Canadian Air Force to offer his services in 1939. But he was rejected due to his lack of academic qualifications. He finally travelled to England to train as an RAF pilot in September 1941 and showed exceptional talent. He had brilliant eyesight which helped him fly, aim and shoot all in one action. He flew his first combat mission on Christmas Day 1941 with 403 Squadron stationed at North Weald in Essex.

Volunteering for an overseas posting, Beurling landed on Malta on 9 June 1942. Squadron Commander 'Laddie' Lucas later spoke of his first impression of Beurling on arrival at the airbase: 'I felt I was in the presence of a very unusual young man. He didn't give a damn for me. A youngster really, who was champing at the bit to get to it, to get in an aeroplane and have a go.'

In more ways than one, Beurling flew straight into the thick of the action on 12 June 1942. His formation of Spitfires engaged eight German Bf 109s in the skies over Malta and he claimed a kill. Unverified by anyone else flying that day, Beurling was infuriated when his 'Kill' was downgraded to a 'Damaged'. He went on to cut his combat teeth against the experienced and numerous German Aces that assaulted Malta day and night in 1942. However, nine of his kills on Malta were Italian pilots about whom he said, 'The Jerries are probably better over-all pilots than the Italians but they certainly let the Eyeties do their fighting for them when the going gets tough'.

Beurling soon established himself as the star pilot of his squadron.

His 'Buzz' and 'Screwball' nicknames (screwball due to his use of the word to describe almost every living thing), were soon joined by a grander soubriquet. Due to his hunter instinct and sharp eyes he became known as 'The Falcon of Malta'. Beurling's ruthless-assassin personality comes across loud and clear, when he speaks of the thrill of air combat in press interviews.

One of my cannon shells caught him in the face and blew his head right off. The body slumped and the slipstream caught the stub of the neck, and the blood streamed down the side of the cockpit. It was a great sight ... red blood down the white fuselage. I must say it gives you a feeling of satisfaction when you actually blow their brains out.

After two months on Malta he had amassed a personal tally of 16 enemy planes destroyed and five damaged. A

Distinguished Service Order (DSO) award followed, but a severe bout of dysentery prevented further flights for much of the rest of his time on the island. Even so, his score on Malta rose to 27 kills, the highest of any RAF pilot during the campaign. In achieving that total he was shot down four times. Due to his exceptional courage in combat and unparalleled flying skills, he secured his final and most distinguished *nom de guerre*. Named after the religious fighting order of medieval knights who had protected Malta against invasion in the sixteenth century, Buzz Beurling became 'The Knight of Malta'.

In September 1943, Beurling transferred to the Royal Canadian Air Force which had so painfully snubbed him four years earlier. But he was wild and didn't settle. His superiors were horrified at his lack of discipline, he flew too fast and refused to stay in formation. Eventually he was grounded, and despite a later attempt to join the United States Air Force, Beurling's wartime ended with an honorable discharge. His strike tally during World War II was a total of 31 kills and one shared, plus nine damaged. He was also awarded a DSO, a DFC and a Distinguished Flying Medal (DFM) with bar.

Finding it difficult to adjust to civilian life, Beurling was recruited to fly P-51 Mustangs for the Israeli Air Force, but he was killed in a crash during a test flight at Rome airport in May 1948, when he was only 26 years old. It was his tenth crash, and many said the devil that had been chasing his tail had finally caught up with Buzz Beurling. His old mentor, Group Captain Laddie Lucas gave an astute understated appraisal of the Knight of Malta — 'penetrating blue eyes … highly strung and outspoken … something of a rebel'.

(Left) Buzz Beurling adds another German 'kill' insignia to his Spitfire; (right) the crest of 403 Squadron.

THE BATTLE OF EL ALAMEIN

DATELINE ... 23 OCTOBER 1942 ... 11 NOVEMBER 1942

The 'Desert Fox', Field Marshal Erwin Rommel was on the run in the deserts of North Africa. The two battles fought near El Alamein on the Mediterranean coast of Egypt, 250 miles (400 km) west of the Suez Canal, marked a major turning point in World War II. The first battle stalled the advance of the Axis forces through North Africa. The second, between 23 October and 11 November 1942, saw General Bernard Montgomery's British 8th Army driving back Rommel's *Afrika Korps* and ending Axis hopes of taking control of the Suez Canal and the oil fields of the Middle East. While the Battle of El Alamein is generally thought of as a tank battle, air support proved to be a

A Curtiss P-40 ready for take off, North Africa, 1942.

vital factor in the eventual Allied victory. At El Alamein that support was provided by the 'Cinderella' squadrons of World War II, the Desert Air Force.

The Desert Air Force

From the very outbreak of war, protecting Britain was the RAF's top priority, and so the Desert Air Force (DAF) of North Africa had to make do with cast-offs, limited resources and older aircraft such as the Gloster Gladiator biplane fighter and Bristol Blenheim bomber. Despite this, the DAF initially scored notable successes over the Italian Air Force – not least because it was also equally poorly equipped. The reinforcement of Italian positions with German armaments and aircraft, however, posed a new threat to the British North African positions and the Ministry of War in London eventually began to make Hawker Hurricanes available.

In 1941, the Curtiss P-40 was also used very effectively in combat operations in North Africa. However, once the immediate Nazi threat to the British Isles had passed in 1942, Supermarine Spitfires arrived, and began to transform the Allied aerial threat in the skies over North Africa. The arrival of new aircraft undoubtedly re-energized the DAF, but perhaps the most significant factor in the success of the force lay in a gradual tactical change as crews became experienced in overcoming the unique challenges of desert warfare.

> "... Before Alamein we never had a victory. After Alamein we never had a defeat ..."
>
> Winston Churchill

The Battle of El Alamein

The Luftwaffe had long been used as a type of 'flying artillery' by the *Wehrmacht* and the DAF adapted this idea by using 'Forward Air Controllers' attached to Army units to call in air support when needed. 'Cab ranks' of fighter-bombers circled in the air awaiting a radio call to attack a given target. It meant that aircraft could be deployed quickly and accurately, and the results were so impressive that a similar system would later be used during the D-Day landings of Operation Overlord in 1944.

When the Americans reinforced the DAF in the form of 12th Bombardment Group and 57th Fighter Group, they immediately adopted these tactics. Cooperation between the British and Americans reached hitherto unparalleled levels and by late 1942 the two air forces were essentially a joint rapid-response resource capable of flexible deployment to an ever-changing schedule of priority trouble spots.

The End Of The Beginning

By 2 November 1942, Rommel knew that he was in serious trouble. The battle had swung back and forth as each side attacked and counter-attacked, but the British under Montgomery had had the best of it. Lack of supplies meant that the Desert Fox could no longer see a way to win the battle, and he considered that his best hope lay in an orderly withdrawal so his battered forces could regroup and launch a new offensive at a later point.

CURTISS P-40

The P-40 was an all-American, all-metal, single-seat fighter built in 1938. The United States makers Curtiss used the name Warhawk, but the British and Commonwealth air forces knew the plane as the Tomahawk. P-40s first flew combat service missions for the British Commonwealth squadrons of the Desert Air Force in the North African campaigns during June 1941. The RAF pilots of Squadron 112 were the first to fly Tomahawks in North Africa and was also the first Allied unit to paint the 'shark's mouth' logo on the nose of their aircraft, after personally witnessing similar aggressive markings on the Luftwaffe fighters. High altitude combat in Europe could end in death and disaster as the P-40s could be easily outmaneuvered by Luftwaffe fighters such as the Messerschmitt Bf 109. But between 1941 and 1944, P-40 Tomahawks played a critical role with the Allied air forces in North Africa where high altitude performance was less crucial.

THE SKIES OF THE MEDITERRANEAN AND NORTH AFRICA

The army's strength was so exhausted after its ten days of battle that it was not now capable of offering any effective opposition to the enemy's next breakthrough attempt … With our great shortage of vehicles an orderly withdrawal of the non-motorized forces appeared impossible … In these circumstances we had to reckon, at the least, with the gradual destruction of the army.

Generalfeldmarschall Erwin Rommel
Commander of the Afrika Korps

Hitler responded by ordering Rommel to fight on. Fearing a renewed attack the next day might decimate his precious *Afrika Korps*, Rommel withdrew them and left the X and XXI Italian Corps, supported by the 90th Light Division, to try and hold the line. On 3 November 1942, the massive attack that Rommel had feared duly arrived. It was the busiest day of the battle for the Desert Air Force, which flew a total of 1,208 sorties against the Axis positions. In a little under 24 hours, the DAF bombers dropped almost 400 tons of bombs, fatally weakening the Italians' ability to fight on.

Rommel fled further backwards and Montgomery was forced to pause his pursuit in order to allow his supply lines to catch up. The geographic spread of the various retreating *Afrika Korps* divisions made it difficult for the DAF to make much impression on them, though they harried them as best they could. US bombers struck at Tobruk and Benghazi, sinking Axis ships and tankers to compound Rommel's misery. By the time the German commander reached the relative safety of Tripoli, he had just 80 tanks left, and in excess of 40,000 Axis troops had been killed, wounded or taken captive.

The Germans have received back again that measure of fire and steel which they have so often meted out to others. Now, this is not the end. It is not even the beginning of the end. But it is, perhaps, the end of the beginning.

British Prime Minister Winston S. Churchill
Westminster, London, 1942

Africa Korps in discussion, on a North African air base, 1941.

ROMMEL VS MONTGOMERY

The Desert Fox

Erwin Johannes Eugen Rommel

15 November 1891 — 14 October 1944

Born: Heidenheim, Württemberg, Germany

Rank: Generalfeldmarschall

Rommel fought in World War I on the Italian Front, and commanded the 7th Panzer Division in World War II. He led the charge in the invasion of France in 1940, and commanded the German and Italian forces in North Africa. During 1942 at the Battle of El Alamein he faced Bernard Montgomery's 8th Army for the first time, later commanding the German defending forces against the Allied invasion of Normandy in 1944, Rommel and Montgomery's paths crossed again. He was a well-respected and professional soldier and his *Afrika Korps* were never accused of war crimes. A German hero, Rommel was identified as one of the conspirators in the attempt to assassinate Hitler in July 1944. Seeking retribution, Hitler forced Rommel to commit suicide in return for assurances of his family's safety. His death was officially announced as a heart attack following a car crash, and he was given a full ceremonial funeral.

Monty

Bernard Law Montgomery

17 November 1887 — 24 March 1976

Born: Kennington, London

Rank: Field Marshal

After being wounded in battle as a Captain during World War I, Montgomery commanded the British 8th Army in the Western Desert of North Africa in 1942. At the Battle of El Alamein and the subsequent invasion of Sicily and Italy, his direct opposite number was Erwin Rommel. He was responsible for planning D-Day and commanded the ground forces during Operation Overlord, while Rommel was defending the Normandy coastline. He continued to be in charge of the 21st Army Group for the rest of the Western Europe campaign of World War II and on 4 May 1945 was the Commander-in-Charge who took the German surrender in northern Germany at Lüneburg Heath. After the war, he became Chief of the Imperial General Staff and was appointed Viscount Montgomery of Alamein. He died, aged 88, in 1976. Every year, as a mark of respect, during a remembrance service, a bugler plays the Last Post at his grave in Hampshire, England.

THE
SKIES
OF THE
PACIFIC

PEARL HARBOR

DATELINE ... 7 DECEMBER 1941

The United States was still officially negotiating a non-aggression pact with Japan. Nobody seriously believed that Japan would attack without first issuing a declaration of hostile intent. Japan's previous unannounced acts of war against China in 1895 and Russia in 1905 were considered ancient history. However, with flagrant disregard for the ongoing negotiations and in a shocking act of all-out war, on 7 December 1941 without warning, Pearl Harbor, the headquarters of the United States Pacific Fleet, was bombed by the Imperial Japanese Navy. The outrageous onslaught led directly to the American entry into both the war in the Pacific and the war in Europe.

Expect the Unexpected

It had been an uneventful, sunny Sunday morning for the two young American radar operators. 19-year-old Private Joseph L. Lockard and 23-year-old Private George E. Elliot had been on duty since 04:00 hours, waiting and watching for any movement on the surrounding Pacific Ocean. The brand new Opana Radar Site, south of Kawela Bay on the northern tip of the island of O'ahu, Hawaii, was specifically designed to monitor sea and air activity, providing the American naval base at Pearl Harbor with vital information on the movements of the Imperial Japanese Navy. The truck to take the young soldiers to breakfast was late so they hung around familiarizing themselves with the newly installed equipment. Just after 07:00 hours a huge blip appeared on the screen, suggesting

a large force of aircraft was approaching from the north at a distance of around 130 miles (210 km). The privates relayed their discovery by telephone to a Lieutenant on duty at the Aircraft Warning Service headquarters. He told them not to worry about it. It was probably a flight of American B-17 Flying Fortresses from California. There was no reason for an unexpected Japanese force to be approaching. The brand new system had failed as the early warning of the imminent danger from the two young radar operators went totally unheeded.

Around an hour later the first bombs were falling on Pearl Harbor, as the Japanese planes that Lockard and Elliot had detected, launched the most notorious, and perhaps most significant, single air-attack in history. The assault on the United States Pacific Fleet caused worldwide consternation and immediately threw the mighty resources of the USA into a war against the impressive power of the Japanese Empire.

Devastating Strike Force

Diplomatic tension had been mounting between America and Japan since the start of the Second Sino-Japanese War in 1937. The war with China was a result of decades of Japanese attempts to dominate China politically and militarily to secure access to China's vast raw material and labour resources. By 1940, the United States had become China's main financial backer and military hardware supplier, and Japan's war with China had reached an uneasy stalemate.

Consequently, Japan had embarked on a widespread program of invasion and military expansion throughout the Pacific region, taking control of key geographic locations and threatening vital US trade routes. The American government instigated sanctions against Japan, and international relations between the two countries were at an all-time low.

The audacious plan to strike at Pearl Harbor was the brainchild of Admiral Isoroku Yamamoto, Commander-in-Chief of the Japanese Combined Fleet. His objective was to bomb the US Pacific Fleet out of existence, allowing Japan to continue their imperial invasion operations in the South Seas with impunity.

The Japanese aircraft carriers that brought the attack planes within range of US soil had left their base at Hitokappu Bay at 06:00 hours on 26 November 1941. The force was deliberately kept as small as possible to

(Above) A Japanese Mitsubishi A6M Zero fighter takes off from the aircraft carrier *Akagi*, on its way to attack Pearl Harbor on the morning of 7 December 1941.

Photograph taken from a Japanese plane during the Pearl Harbor attack.
A torpedo has just hit USS *West Virginia* on the far side of Ford Island (center). Other battleships moored nearby are (from left): *Nevada, Arizona, Tennessee, Oklahoma, Maryland,* and *California.* Japanese planes are visible in the right center (over Ford Island) and over the Navy Yard (right).

avoid detection, yet be capable of launching a decisive strike. Six aircraft carriers took part – *Akagi, Kaga, Soryu, Zuikaku, Hiryu* and *Shokaku*. Their own pilots were reinforced with the best and most experienced pilots from other carriers. Months of special training had ensured that all the men involved were in peak condition for the raid. To create total surprise, the fleet passed between Midway and the Aleutian Islands – outside the range of US patrol planes – as well as using submarines as scouts to give advance warning of any enemy ships in the area. Strict radio silence was maintained throughout.

The Natural Lagoon in Paradise

Pearl Harbor is a Pacific Ocean deep-water US naval base, on the Hawaiian island of O'ahu. The United States Pacific Fleet had been moved to Pearl Harbor to demonstrate to the Japanese that America was prepared to use force to defend her interests if needed. Although Hawaii occupies a pivotal position of major strategic significance in the centre of the Pacific Ocean, Pearl Harbor was far from an ideal base. It had never been conceived as a home for such a large fleet, and its narrow entrance to the natural lagoon within gave little leeway for the movement of large ships. As a result, on the morning of 7 December 1941, the harbor was full of tightly packed large vessels, presenting giant unmissable targets to the enemy bombers.

From the Japanese perspective, however, an attack on Pearl Harbor was a formidable challenge. Shallow and narrow, it was not well suited to torpedo attack – yet that was the type of attack likely to cause most damage. It was also thought to be equipped with torpedo nets, which would seriously limit the effectiveness of any payloads dropped. And then, of course, there was the danger posed by the large number of American fighter planes known to be guarding the area.

To overcome the first difficulty, the Japanese fitted their torpedoes with stabilizers and dropped them from extremely low altitude, which prevented them from diving too deeply into the water. To overcome the torpedo nets, secondary dive-bomb and horizontal bombing attacks would be carried out. Neutralizing the threat of the American fighters would be achieved by surprising them before they could get into the air. Japanese dive bombers and fighters planned to attack the American air bases first, and destroy the US fighters on the ground.

Massive Attack

The attack force consisted of 360 planes, which arrived at Pearl Harbor in two waves. The first wave of 189 planes took off at 06:00 hours – just after dawn in order to provide maximum daylight for the operation. It consisted of 50 horizontal bombers, each carrying an 800 kg bomb, 40 torpedo planes carrying similar sized torpedoes, and 54 dive-bombers carrying 250 kg bombs for less well protected ships such as the aircraft carriers and cruisers rather than battleships. Accompanying the force were 45 fighters to strafe enemy positions if no resistance was encountered in the air.

The second wave of 171 planes was scheduled to take off one hour and 15 minutes after the first. It consisted of further horizontal bombers carrying 250 kg and 60 kg bombs, plus torpedo bombers whose targets would be any major ships of the Pacific Fleet that had survived the first wave.

Another 36 fighters would provide cover and strafe US ground crew attempting to repair the damage caused by the earlier attack.

Brilliant Red Sun Insignia

The American fighter bases at Wheeler Field and Ford Island were the first to be hit at around 07:55 hours on the morning of 7 December 1941. The torpedo planes and horizontal bombers struck Pearl Harbor itself just a couple of minutes later. Finding no aircraft carriers present, those pilots carrying the smaller 250kg bombs had no choice but to target them on the battleships. Any concern about the amount of damage they might inflict was more than made up for by the damage caused by the torpedoes however. Dropped from a height of 50 – 100 feet (15 – 30 m) they could not miss their target. Using oxygen rather than air for propulsion, the Japanese torpedoes were more explosive than US versions, and were also much larger. Pearl Harbor did not deploy torpedo nets as the Japanese had feared – the Americans' need to land seaplanes in the harbor precluded their use. The vessels of the American fleet were sitting ducks for the first wave, and the result was devastation on a scale that witnesses could hardly believe. Acting Commanding Officer, Lieutenant Commander S. S. Isquith, provided one of the few survivor's reports from the badly-hit USS *Utah*.

… Three planes whose identification were not questioned but taken for US planes maneuvering, were observed just as colors were being hoisted at 08:00, heading northerly from the harbor entrance. They made a low dive on the southern end of Ford Island and each dropped a bomb. Immediately thereafter the air was filled with planes clearly distinguished as yellow colored planes with brilliant red Rising Sun insignia on fuselage and red wing tips, flying low at about 100 knots speed and dropping aerial torpedoes and bombs … The general alarm was immediately rung and word was passed, 'All hands to bombing quarters.' At about this time, 08:01, a severe underwater hit, at approximately frame 84, port side, was felt and the ship immediately commenced to list to port. Another underwater hit was felt almost immediately thereafter in about the same general location and the listing of the ship increased immediately to about 15 degrees. At this time I realized that the ship would capsize and word was passed. 'All hands on deck and all engine room and fire room, radio and dynamo watch to lay up on deck and release all prisoners.' … Lieutenant P. F. Hauck, Machinist S. A. Szymanski, and myself were the last to leave the ship going through the ports in the Captain's cabin. At this time, about 08:10, the ship was listing about 80 degrees to port and the planes were still strafing the ship. Mooring lines were parting and two motor launches and the motor whale boat were picking up men in the water. Many men were observed swimming to the north and south quays of Pier FOX-11, and as planes were still strafing, the men were ordered to the sides of the quays for some protection.

Lieutenant Commander S. S. Isquith, USS Utah
Pearl Harbor, 7 December 1941

Catastrophic Destruction

After the initial shock of the attack, the ships that had not been damaged beyond repair began to desperately return the fire of the Japanese planes. The USS *Nevada* deserves special mention for firing her guns at 08:02 hours, just a minute after the planes were sighted, and also managing to get underway and head for the harbor entrance. Struck by one torpedo and at least six bombs,

she continued to defend herself and later claimed five enemy aircraft destroyed. Many other crews, however, could only abandon their ships as flames tore through them from repeated direct hits.

There was also chaos and devastation at the airfields. Not expecting attack, the parked US fighter planes were grouped together on the ground more or less wing-tip to wing-tip, making them perfect targets for the Japanese dive-bombers and strafing attacks. Some men did manage to scramble their planes into the sky, and by the end of the attack the Hawaiian Air Force had claimed 10 kills and two damaged. But despite these heroic efforts, the Japanese faced no tangibly serious aerial threat throughout the attack. Their total losses amounted to just 29 planes, the majority of them dive bombers while over 250 US planes were destroyed, either on the ground or shot down.

The damage to the US fleet was equally severe. Eight US battleships were damaged with four being sunk – USS *Arizona*, *California*, *West Virginia* and *Oklahoma* – along with a cruiser and two tankers. The only consolation for the US was that many ships of the fleet were not in the harbor that morning for one reason or another, and the list of those absent included all three of the fleet's aircraft carriers. Nonetheless, the attack crippled both the fleet and its air support, and left over 2,400 people dead, with many more injured.

An hour after the attack, Japanese diplomats passed a communiqué to the US government formally breaking off the non-aggression pact negotiations. The timing was not what Admiral Yamamoto had planned, but the fourteen-part declaration sent to the Japanese ambassador in Washington DC had

taken longer to translate from Japanese than anyone imagined. By the time the message was received, it was too late, the attack was over and the irreparable damage was done.

Obviously it is the intention of the American Government to conspire with Great Britain and other countries to obstruct Japan's effort toward the establishment of peace through the creation of a new order in East Asia, and especially to preserve Anglo-American rights and interest by keeping Japan and China at war. This intention has been revealed clearly during the course of the present negotiation. Thus, the earnest hope of the Japanese Government to adjust Japanese-American relations and to preserve and promote the peace of the Pacific through cooperation with the American Government has finally been lost. The Japanese Government regrets to have to notify hereby the American Government that in view of the attitude of the American Government it cannot but consider that it is impossible to reach an agreement through further negotiations.

Extract from the so-called 'Fourteen Part Message' Communiqué from Japanese Government

American Transformation

Horrifyingly enough, it could have been worse. Had the Japanese pressed home their attack with a third strike they could easily have destroyed key naval installations, oil storage depots and submarine bases as well as finishing off the 38 cruisers and destroyers that survived the first bombs. Moreover, the American aircraft carriers were untouched and, along with US submarines, went on to be more important than any of the damaged American battleships in the future elimination and immobilization of the Imperial Japanese Navy. The survival of the repair yards and oil depots also allowed

(Left) USS *West Virginia* burning in Pearl Harbor.

THE SKIES OF THE PACIFIC

Pearl Harbor to supply continued logistical support to US Naval operations in the Pacific, so essential to the war effort on the islands of the South Pacific and central to the Battles of the Coral Sea and Midway.

The Japanese victory at Pearl Harbor had a massive impact on the outcome of World War II. Japanese commanders had hoped the devastation would demoralize America and dissuade the American public from supporting the war. But they badly misjudged the inner strength and collective outrage of the American people under attack. Firmly united behind President Franklin D. Roosevelt, all talk of appeasement ceased and America declared war on Japan. Galvanized by the injustice of the Japanese surprise attack, America was transformed. Her factories began to produce the materials of war at a prodigious rate. With Germany and Italy declaring war on the USA in support of Japan, thousands of loyal Americans rushed to sign up for military service, creating a sudden massive injection of fresh young manpower and heavy weaponry heading for the war in Europe as well as the Pacific. World War II drastically altered the lives of men and women across the globe. However, from the very beginning, President Franklin D. Roosevelt was resolute. His ultimate single demand from the Japanese Empire was made abundantly clear – Unconditional Surrender. Nothing less would do.

> "...With the unbounded determination of our people – we will gain the inevitable triumph – so help us God ..."

Yesterday, December 7, 1941 – a date which will live in infamy – the United States of America was suddenly and deliberately attacked by naval and air forces of the Empire of Japan. The United States was at peace with that nation and, at the solicitation of Japan, was still in conversation with its Government and its Emperor looking toward the maintenance of peace in the Pacific ... The facts of yesterday speak for themselves. The people of the United States have already formed their opinions and well understand the implications to the very life and safety of our nation. As Commander-in-Chief of the Army and Navy, I have directed that all measures be taken for our defense. Always will we remember the character of the onslaught against us. No matter how long it may take us to overcome this premeditated invasion, the American people in their righteous might will win through to absolute victory.

I believe I interpret the will of the Congress and of the people when I assert that we will not only defend ourselves to the uttermost, but will make very certain that this form of treachery shall never endanger us again. Hostilities exist. There is no blinking at the fact that our people, our territory and our interests are in grave danger. With confidence in our armed forces – with the unbounded determination of our people – we will gain the inevitable triumph – so help us God. I ask that the Congress declare that since the unprovoked and dastardly attack by Japan on Sunday, December 7th, a state of war has existed between the United States and the Japanese Empire.

US President Franklin D. Roosevelt
Address to US Congress, 8 December 1941

140

(Right above) Hiroyoshi Nishizawa; (right) A6M Zero, flown by Hiroyoshi Nishizawa over the Solomon Islands, 1943.

JAPAN'S ACE OF ACES
HIROYOSHI NISHIZAWA

Hiroyoshi Nishizawa did not look like a military hero, suffering constantly from malaria and skin diseases. He was taller than most Japanese, but at 5 ft 8 in (1.73 m) and weighing 140 pounds (64 kg) he was an ideal size for a fighter pilot. Once inside the cockpit of his Mitsubishi A6M Zero, he became a deadly assassin.

Responsible for at least 87 kills, Nishizawa, wreaked havoc among the Australian and United States Air Forces as they attempted to establish air superiority in the Pacific War. All those who flew with him and against him agreed that he was a pilot of exceptional talent, and his aerobatic techniques during aerial combat astonished and inspired lesser pilots to match his skill.

But glory days for Japanese Aces were short-lived, as more and more USAAF aircraft entered the Pacific War and their skilful young American pilots gradually gained vital combat experience. Nishizawa lost several close friends and was himself shot down.

In February 1943, the last Japanese troops were withdrawn from Guadalcanal and Nishizawa, by then on around 50 kills, could see that the tide of the battle was turning. After another year of valiant combat missions, he had a premonition that death was close at hand, and volunteered for a *Kamikaze* suicide mission.

His offer was refused on the grounds that he was too valuable an asset for Japan to lose. He was instead ordered to pick up and transport new Zero fighters from Clark Field on the island of Luzon in the Philippines. Whilst en route, the bomber he was a passenger in was shot down by US Hellcats from the carrier USS *Wasp*, and Nishizawa was killed. Japan's greatest ever Ace was posthumously given the name *Bukai-in Kohan Giko Kyoshi* — In the ocean of the military, reflective of all distinguished pilots, an honoured Buddhist person.

MITSUBISHI A6M ZERO

Zeroes were the long range carrier fighter aircraft flown by the Japanese in the attack on Pearl Harbor. With a similar radial engine to the German Focke-Wulf 190 and a massive range of 1,600 miles (2,560 km), the A6M had a top speed of 370 mph. Christened the 'Zero' by its opponents, after its Japanese Naval designation 'Navy Type 0 Carrier Fighter', Japanese fighter pilots called it the *Zero-sen*, while the name used in USAAF flying reports was the 'Zeke'.

Every possible weight-saving measure had been incorporated into the manufacture of the A6M by the Mitsubishi designers to increase the aircraft's dynamics — speed, range and mobility were the key features of any fighter plane and Mitsubishi were under strict government instructions to produce the best ever made. Designed with a short wing-span to take up less space on board an aircraft carrier, the new Zeroes that came off the production lines were regarded as the ultimate fighting machines. From its introduction to the Imperial Japanese Navy in 1940 and 1942, the Zeke was the most agile fighter plane in the world, and when the Pacific War broke out it soon gained a reputation as a legendary dogfighter.

As USAAF tactics improved, however, and US manufacturers increased the speed, firepower and mobility of their aircraft, the vulnerabilities of the largely unmodified Zero were eventually exposed, but the A6M was never replaced by newer Japanese aircraft. US Pilots learned to avoid the Japanese fighters in dogfights and instead swooped down from above, attempting to shoot down the Zero in a single pass before returning to the relative safety of high altitude.

Over 11,000 Zeroes were produced making it without question the most important Japanese plane throughout the war, accounting for over 1,500 USAAF planes. In the closing stages of the Pacific War, Zeroes were used to deadly effect in *Kamikaze* missions, the suicide crash-dive attacks flown by the Japanese pilots against US Navy vessels.

THE DOOLITTLE RAID

DATELINE ... 1 APRIL 1942 ... 18 APRIL 1942

Capturing the prevailing global mood of the time, the tone of the mission statement issued by the newly-formed United Nations on 1 January 1942, was one of grim determination. Morale had reached an all-time low in the countries facing the overwhelming force of Germany, Italy and Japan. For the nations embroiled in the conflict, united in adversity, it was perhaps the darkest of all the many dark hours of World War II.

The Doolittle Tokyo Raid

There was little reason for the populations of the United Kingdom, United States of America or USSR to celebrate as the clock struck midnight on 1 January 1942. All three countries were now at war, and all three knew that the war was not going well for them. The UK had resisted invasion, but had been forced into humiliating retreats in the Mediterranean, North Africa and the Far East. The Soviet Union had halted the initial blitzkrieg of Operation Barbarossa,

but German forces remained poised to attack Moscow and had a vice-like grip on Leningrad, which was being slowly starved to death. The United States was still in shock and reeling after the devastating Japanese attack on Pearl Harbor. It was against this backdrop, in retribution for the Pearl Harbor attack, that President Franklin D. Roosevelt and the United States Joint Chiefs of Staff devised an audacious plan to bomb the Japanese capital city of Tokyo.

The two-fold objective of the raid would be to boost the morale of the American people and to demonstrate to the Japanese that their homeland was far from invulnerable. Navy Captain Francis Low came up with the concept that United States medium-range

THE GOVERNMENTS SIGNATORY HERETO,

Having subscribed to a common program of purposes and principles embodied in the Joint Declaration of the President of the United States of America and the Prime Minister of the United Kingdom of Great Britain and Northern Ireland dated August 14, 1941, known as the Atlantic Charter. Being convinced that complete victory over their enemies is essential to defend life, liberty, independence and religious freedom, and to preserve human rights and justice in their own lands as well as in other lands, and that they are now engaged in a common struggle against savage and brutal forces seeking to subjugate the world,

DECLARE:

(1) Each Government pledges itself to employ its full resources, military or economic, against those members of the Tripartite Pact and its adherents with which such government is at war.

(2) Each Government pledges itself to cooperate with the Governments signatory hereto and not to make a separate armistice or peace with the enemies.

The foregoing declaration may be adhered to by other nations which are, or which may be, rendering material assistance and contributions in the struggle for victory over Hitlerism.

DONE at Washington

January First, 1942

Pamphlet No. 4, Pillars of Peace. Documents Pertaining To American Interest In Establishing A Lasting World Peace: January 1941–February 1946

(Above) UN Mission Statement, 1942.

(Left) B-25 Mitchell bombers on the flight deck of USS *Hornet* on their way to Tokyo to take part in the Doolittle Raid 1942.

bombers could take off from US aircraft carriers that had sailed within flying range of Japan. Having successfully struck their targets in Tokyo, the bombers would then continue westward to land in the territory of the US ally, China. The man selected to plan and lead the retaliatory mission, Lieutenant Colonel James Doolittle, later outlined the goals in his retrospective official report. Several quotes from Doolittle's report are used below to help narrate the epic story of the raid.

The object of the project was to bomb the industrial centers of Japan. It was hoped that the damage done would be both material and psychological. Material damage was to be the destruction of specific targets with ensuing confusion and retardation of production. The psychological results, it was hoped, would be the recalling of combat equipment from other theaters for home defense thus effecting relief in those theaters, the development of a fear complex in Japan, improved relationships with our Allies, and a favorable reaction on the American people.

Lieutenant Colonel James Doolittle, Report to General H.H. Arnold, Commanding General of US Army Air Forces, 9 July 1942

No Shortage of Volunteers

The mission was both ambitious and highly risky. Doolittle sought volunteers from the 17th Bomber Group, who were already experienced in flying the intended mission aircraft, the North American B-25 Mitchell twin-engined medium bomber. Every man in the Bomber Group put their name forward. James Doolittle and the 80 elite airmen he selected to fly the sixteen B-25 Mitchells on this nationally significant mission became known as the Doolittle Raiders.

With his team chosen Doolittle analyzed the many formidable logistical obstacles he needed to overcome to ensure the raid's success. First and foremost, the B-25 Mitchell was never designed to take off from an aircraft carrier. The latest standard production model, the B-25B, required a runway of at least 1,250 ft (380 m) to get into the air. If Doolittle wanted to launch a bomb-carrying aircraft from a carrier, he had to find a way to get airborne from the available 500 ft (150 m) of carrier deck. The ship could be rolling in high seas, and top-heavy from the added weight of the 16 aircraft and their lethal cargo. Each aircraft would carry four specially made 500 lb (225 kg) bombs. It had never been attempted before, and there were plenty who doubted that it was possible.

Every superfluous item was stripped from the aircraft, including the radios. Extra fuel tanks were installed, along with dummy wooden tail guns to fool enemy fighters into not attacking the exposed rears of the planes. The aircraft carrier selected for the mission, USS *Hornet*, put to sea with a single modified B-25 on board to test whether a carrier take-off would be possible. It was very close, but the B-25 made it into the air. The doubters had been silenced.

The 16 B-25 bombers and their five-man crews were loaded on board the USS *Hornet* on 1 April 1942. The wingspan of the B-25s meant they had to be transported on the flight deck with the *Hornet's* fighters stowed below. Leaving the port of Alameda in California on 2 April, the heavily-laden *Hornet* sailed to meet a US Navy Task Force assembled near Hawaii, comprising the aircraft carrier USS *Enterprise* and a protective escort of cruisers and destroyers. On 17 April 1942, the assembled vessels, designated as Task Force

16, carried James Doolittle and his Doolittle Raiders through the Japanese-controlled waters of the west Pacific to deliver America's deadly answer to the Japanese attack on Pearl Harbor directly into the heart of Tokyo.

As Far West As Possible

After take-off it was planned that the pilots needed to conserve as much fuel as possible during their journey. Even with the extra petrol tanks fitted, it was debatable whether the bombers could make it safely all the way to the scheduled landing field in China without running out of fuel. That aspect of the task was made increasingly difficult when a Japanese picket boat sighted the US fleet at 07:38 hours on the morning of 18 April 1942, the *Hornet* was still some 640 nautical miles from Japan – 170 miles (275 km) further away from the targets than planned.

Although the patrol boat was rapidly sunk, it had time to send a warning message to Tokyo, and so a decision had to be made to abandon the mission or attempt to launch the aircraft from the present location. It was simply too dangerous for the fleet to press on into hostile waters now that it had been discovered. Doolittle decided to go for it. With a little luck, he figured the B-25s could still get close enough to China for the crews to bail out somewhere near to the shore.

Final instructions were to avoid non-military targets, particularly the Temple of Heaven, and even though we were put off so far at sea that it would be impossible to reach the China Coast, not to go to Siberia but to proceed as far West as possible, land on the water, launch the rubber boat and sail in.

Lieutenant Colonel James Doolittle, Report to General H.H. Arnold, Commanding General of US Army Air Forces, 9 July 1942

Despite none of the pilots ever having taken off from a carrier before, all 16 planes made it into the air safely. They flew at low level towards Japan, arriving over Tokyo around six hours later, at noon local time. To the amazement of Doolittle and the bomber crews, they encountered no enemy fighters en route, and only light anti-aircraft fire as they flew across their targets.

All but one of the bombers managed to find their targets and release their payloads. The one bomber that didn't reach the target had to ditch its bombs in the sea after running into a swarm of fighters. Although the rest of the aircraft did see enemy fighters in the sky, few of them attacked and those that did attack seemed wary of getting too close to the B-25's defensive guns.

The best information available from Army and Navy intelligence sources indicates that there were some 500 combat planes in Japan and that most of them were concentrated in the Tokyo Bay area. The comparatively few fighters encountered indicated that home defense had been reduced in the interest of making the maximum of planes available in active theaters. The pilots of such planes as remained appeared inexperienced. In some cases they actually did not attack, and in many cases failed to drive the attack home to the maximum extent possible ... The fire of the pilots that actually attacked was very inaccurate.

Lieutenant Colonel James Doolittle, Report to General H.H. Arnold, Commanding General of US Army Air Forces, 9 July 1942

Completing the Mission

Against the odds, 17th Bomber Group had succeeded in striking back at Japan. Now came the second part of the job – trying to get home. All of the planes were critically short of fuel by now, so were anxiously scanning the ground for any signs of homing beacons as they moved south-west from the coast of Japan and across the East China Sea. But no one had told the Chinese at the landing fields in Zhejiang province that the US bombers were on their way. It had been considered too dangerous for the US fleet to break radio silence, and by the time the message was sent to China, it could not be relayed to those tasked with guiding the bombers and they thought they were under attack.

... when our planes were heard overhead an air raid warning alarm was sounded and lights were turned off. This, together with the very unfavorable flight weather over the China Coast, made safe landing at destination impossible. As a result all planes either landed either near the Coast or the crews bailed out with their parachutes.

Lieutenant Colonel James Doolittle, Report to General H.H. Arnold, Commanding General of US Army Air Forces, 9 July 1942

Crash Landings and Capture

While 15 of the bombers flew south-west as planned towards eastern China, the B-25 of Captain Edward J. York, was suffering so badly from a shortage of fuel that reaching the Chinese mainland was impossible. Against instructions, York headed instead towards Siberia and the closer land mass of the Soviet Union. Signatories of a neutrality pact with Japan, Russia had already refused landing permission for the American mission. Because of its proximity, Vladivostok in Siberia had been an early suggestion as a possible landing site in one of Doolittle's draft versions of the raid plans, but Soviet political non-cooperation had meant that

ultimately China, a further 600 miles (970 km), was the final destination.

The other crews crash-landed on Chinese beaches or bravely bailed out as close as possible to shore. They had been flying for 13 hours and had covered a distance of 2,250 miles (3,620 km). Captain York and his crew landed near Vladivostok in the Russian Far Eastern region of Primorsky Krai, bordering China and North Korea. They were imprisoned by the Soviet authorities and had their B-25 confiscated. They spent a year in custody as the Soviets pondered how to release them without violating their neutrality pact with Japan. Eventually the Soviet Secret Police arranged release using a cover story of a bribe being paid to a band of smugglers, and they reached the safety of the British Consulate on 11 May 1943.

The majority of those that landed in China received a hero's welcome from Chinese soldiers and civilians alike, and were rapidly helped to return to the United States. Doolittle himself parachuted from his B-25 and landed in a paddy field near Chuchow. Others were not so fortunate. Corporal Leland D. Faktor died after jumping from his plane, probably due to a heavy landing. Ten other men were missing. It later transpired that two had drowned, and the other eight had fallen into the hands of the Japanese. A war crimes trial after the end of the war would reveal their fate. Three were shot after a 'show-trial' found them guilty of strafing civilians, and the other five were detained in appalling conditions in Japanese prisoner of war camps. They were finally released by American troops in August 1945.

(Right above) Map showing the flight paths and crash sites of the Doolittle Raid, 1942.
(Below) A B-25 takes off from USS *Hornet*.

GENERAL JIMMY DOOLITTLE

James H. Doolittle was a trail-blazing American aviator who earned the Medal of Honor for his leadership of the USAAF Doolittle Raid on Tokyo during World War II.

Doolittle began his flying career enlisting as a cadet in 1917 during World War I, but never left America. He returned to active service as a Major on 1 July 1940 and was promoted to Lieutenant Colonel to lead the first US retaliatory raid on Japan in 1942 after the Pearl Harbor attack. Following the success of the Tokyo raid, Doolittle was promoted by two grades to Brigadier General and in 1943 he was appointed commanding general of the unified USAAF and RAF in the North African campaign.

From January 1944 to September 1945 he commanded the US 8th Air Force in England and contributed significantly to the eventual Allied European air supremacy by instructing US fighters to depart from their bomber escort duties to attack German airfields and transport systems. The 8th Air Force was due to be redeployed to the Pacific in February 1946, but by then the war was over, and Doolittle reverted to inactive reserve status.

In 1951 Doolittle was made a special civilian consultant to the Chief of Staff of the Air Force. He retired in 1959. The General James H. Doolittle Center was opened in 2007 to house the new HQ of 12th Air Force Combined Air Operations in Tucson, Arizona. Surviving Doolittle Raiders attended the inauguration ceremony.

Jimmy Doolittle died in 1993, aged 96, in California and is buried at Arlington National Cemetery, Washington DC. In a final salute to this great warrior a single B-25 Mitchell flew over his grave during the funeral service.

Repercussion and Consequences

James Doolittle initially believed that he would face court-martial for the apparent failure of the mission. All the aircraft had been destroyed, and only light damage had been caused to the targets. In the event, he was fêted as a hero, promoted to Brigadier General and awarded the Medal of Honor. All 80 of the Doolittle Raiders were awarded the Distinguished Flying Cross.

Although he didn't know it at the time, Doolittle's Tokyo Raid had a far greater impact on the outcome of World War II than simply raising the spirits of the American public. To protect Japan from future attack, Admiral Isoroku Yamamoto decided to extend his defensive eastern perimeter by capturing Midway Island, leading to one of the most significant battles of the Pacific War. Imperial Japanese Navy forces including their powerful aircraft carriers were recalled from the Indian Ocean, where they had threatened British shipping and Royal Air Force airfields, in order to fortify Japan itself. No longer did the Japanese feel as though Japan was beyond the reach of Allied air and sea power.

The consequences of the raid for the Chinese were, at least in the short term, catastrophic. In order to avenge China's role in the raid and dissuade future Sino-American cooperation, the Japanese began their notorious Zhejiang-Jiangxi Campaign. They destroyed airfields and used germ warfare in addition to conventional weapons of war to kill an estimated 250,000 civilians during their murderous hunt for the Doolittle crews. This brutal response served to further harden the resolve of the Allies to ensure that such a tyrannical regime be challenged with all the force they could muster. The Doolittle Raid demonstrated that no nation on earth could feel truly safe when at war with an enemy who possessed a powerful air force. Japan, more than any other nation, would come to learn the full consequences of that terrible truth in the years to come.

USAAF Lt. Robert L. Hite captured by the Japanese after the Doolittle Raid.

NORTH AMERICAN
B-25 MITCHELL

The B-25 Mitchell was a twin-engined, medium bomber manufactured by North American Aviation which saw widespread service with many of the Allied air forces in World War II. Named in tribute to General Billy Mitchell, a famous American aviator, nearly 10,000 B-25s were built during four decades of flying.

First coming to prominence as the bomber of the Doolittle Raid, the majority of B-25s were originally used in the Pacific War as strategic bombers, sinking many ships. But in the island-hopping, jungle warfare world of Guam and Guadalcanal, with its two nose-mounted forward-firing machine guns, manned fuselage gun turrets, tail gunner station and superb low altitude flying performance, the B-25 was soon transformed into a hard-hitting ground-attack gunship.

During the North African campaign, B-25s took part as heavily armed low-flying attack aircraft at the Battle of El Alamein, and the subsequent invasion of Italy. A big crowd-pleaser, today, many collectors and aviation museums keep well-maintained B-25s for exhibitions, flying displays and WWII air shows.

THE BATTLE OF MIDWAY

It began with a plea for fresh water. The message from the United States base on Midway Island, stating that its water distillation plant had been damaged, was intercepted by the Japanese, just as US code-breakers had intended. When Japanese communication traffic began to include information that target 'AF' was short of water, US Intelligence was able to confirm that 'AF' was Midway. The JN-25 code had been broken several months earlier, and the US had long known that a major attack was planned for 4 June. Thanks to the carefully planted bogus message from Midway, they now knew not only when the attack would take place, but where. The Japanese hunters were about to become the hunted.

Return of the Ghost Ship

Japanese intelligence stated that the aircraft carrier USS *Yorktown* was lying at the bottom of the Coral Sea off the north-east coast of Australia, having been sunk by a direct hit from a Japanese Aichi D3A a month earlier. It therefore had no business emerging from Pearl Harbor Naval Shipyard on 30 May.

The overenthusiastic claims of Japanese pilots, combined with a miraculous 72 hours of round the clock repairs by US maintenance workers, had created a 'ghost carrier' that should not have been at sea. It meant that the four large aircraft carriers of the Japanese fleet would square up against not two US carriers, but three. Or four, if Midway Island itself is included – as it perhaps should be, given that it was rapidly reinforced with planes, and thus became an unsinkable aircraft carrier in the middle of the Pacific Ocean.

The United States was still outnumbered and outgunned by the Japanese fleet, but it had a much stronger force in the Pacific than the Commander-in-Chief of the Combined Fleet, Admiral Isoroku Yamamoto, realized. His intention was to destroy the US Navy to safeguard Japan against any future repeat of the Doolittle Raid. His complicated plan involved luring the US fleet into open battle at Midway, then using his vastly superior fleet's full strength to sink as many US carriers as possible. But it was Yamamoto who was sailing into a trap, not the US fleet.

Yamamoto's opposite number, American Admiral Chester Nimitz, was aware of the entire Japanese battle plan, which included a simultaneous attack on the Alaskan coast, and could thus secretly place his own fleet in the perfect position for an ambush. Knowing that Yamamoto had divided his fleet into four separate task forces, Nimitz focused on destroying the carrier group, commanded by Vice-Admiral Chuichi Nagumo.

Big Ships, Big Sea

At 04:30 hours on 4 June 1942, Nagumo launched a major attack on Midway as planned. His air force caused significant damage to the base, but failed to disable its airfield. Nagumo resolved to arm his remaining planes with standard bombs designed to strike land targets, with a view to attacking Midway again. At 07:20 hours,

an astonished Japanese scout plane reported a sighting of a US carrier close to Nagumo's fleet. The news threw the Admiral into indecisive confusion.

With half his planes due to return from the first Midway attack, Nagumo had to proceed with the second attack or make ready defensive fighters and torpedo planes to take on the US aircraft carrier. In the event he did not realize the reality of the situation. The US had an entire fleet of carriers at sea, not just one, and each of them had already put its planes into the sky. US fighters, bombers and torpedo planes would shortly arrive to attack the Japanese carriers.

Despite detailed intelligence, there was confusion on the American side too. Due to navigational errors, the planes arrived at their target at different times. The torpedo bombers were first on the scene, and they attacked the carriers as per their orders. With no fighter cover to protect them, however, they were decimated by the Mitsubishi Zeroes of the Japanese air combat patrol. The squadron sent by HMS *Hornet* was almost entirely obliterated. 29 out of the 30 pilots on the mission were killed. The *Yorktown's* squadron lost 21 of the 24 men sent, and the *Enterprise's* squadron lost 18 out of the 28 men sent. In addition, not a single torpedo struck any of the Japanese carriers.

(Above) US Douglas SBD-3 Dauntless dive bombers attack the Japanese fleet during the Battle of Midway, 1942. In the background is a burning Japanese vessel, the *Mikuma*.

Turning the Tide of War

It appeared that the US had managed to snatch defeat from the jaws of victory in the Battle of Midway. But just as Nagumo's fighters were finishing off the US torpedo bombers, dive bombers from the USS *Enterprise* finally located the carriers. They had followed a Japanese destroyer which was steaming to Nagumo's aid. With the Zeroes still out of position the carriers were horribly exposed. The decks of the giant carriers, painted bright yellow and still covered with explosives, fuel and armed torpedo planes, were the perfect targets for the bombers' payloads.

Within just a couple of minutes, the *Kaga* and *Akagi* were blown out of the water. The bombers from the 'ghost carrier' *Yorktown* arrived shortly afterwards and delivered a similar deadly blow to the carrier *Soryu*. The remaining carrier *Hiryu* launched a successful counter-attack and managed to damage the *Yorktown* badly. But soon the *Hiryu* too was found by the US dive bombers and sunk.

What remained of Admiral Yamamoto's force retreated, and the Americans chose not to pursue them. The *Yorktown* was sunk by a Japanese submarine and the Americans claimed a further Japanese cruiser, but the main battle was over. In total the Japanese lost four carriers and a cruiser, against American losses of one carrier. The Japanese dead numbered 3,500 against US losses of 100 men. In addition Japan lost 270 aircraft, against 130 on the US side.

Midway Island remained in US hands and the Japanese combined fleet had been dealt a shattering blow. As well as the crucial carriers, many of Japan's most highly trained airmen, sailors, mechanics and technicians were lost. In retrospect, it was such a catastrophic defeat for Japan that many historians point to the Battle of Midway as the moment when the entire tide of the Pacific War turned.

Crew members examine the damage done to the aircraft carrier, USS *Yorktown* by the Japanese air raiders during the Battle of Midway.

SKIES OVER GUADALCANAL
JOE FOSS AND HIS FLYING CIRCUS

A South Dakota farm boy who waited on tables in order to pay his way through flying school, Joseph Foss rose to become one of America's most respected and highly decorated pilots of World War II. Considered too old for fighter pilot duty at the age of 26 when America joined the war, Foss was initially assigned to a photographic reconnaissance role. He longed for a more exciting and aggressive role however, and in July 1942 his persistent pleas were rewarded with a transfer to Marine Fighting Squadron 121.

As the lead pilot of a group of eight F4F Wildcats, Foss gained a reputation for highly aggressive close-in tactics when engaging the enemy. He and his group became known as the 'Flying Circus' and between them they accounted for 72 Japanese aircraft. Foss himself became America's first 'Ace of Aces' in World War II by destroying at least 23 enemy planes in the brutal daily battles during the Guadalcanal Campaign in 1942–3 for which he was awarded the Medal of Honor from President Franklin D. Roosevelt.

After the war, Foss embarked on a successful career as a Republican governor, before becoming the first Commissioner of the newly-created American Football league in 1959. He died aged 87, in 2003 after a stroke.

For outstanding heroism and courage above and beyond the call of duty as Executive Officer of Marine Fighting Squadron 121, at Guadalcanal, Solomon Islands. Engaging in almost daily combat with the enemy from October 9 to November 19, 1942, Captain Foss personally shot down 23 Japanese aircraft and damaged others so severely that their destruction was extremely probable. In addition, during this period, he successfully led a large number of escort missions, skilfully covering reconnaissance, bombing and photographic planes as well as surface craft. On January 15, 1943, he added three more enemy aircraft to his already brilliant successes for a record of aerial combat achievement unsurpassed in this war. Boldly searching out an approaching enemy force on January 25, Captain Foss led his eight F4F Marine planes and four Army P-38s into action and, undaunted by tremendously superior numbers, intercepted and struck with such force that four Japanese fighters were shot down and the bombers were turned back without releasing a single bomb. His remarkable flying skill, inspiring leadership and indomitable fighting spirit were distinctive factors in the defense of strategic American positions on Guadalcanal.

Major Joseph J Foss, USAAF
Medal of Honor Citation, 18 May 1943

SKIES OF NEW GUINEA

DATELINE ... 3 APRIL 1943 ... 18 APRIL 1943

It was meant to be a birthday present. On 3 April 1943, Admiral Yamamoto flew to the Japanese base at Rabaul in New Guinea to supervise Operation 'I-Go', the massive attack planned to coincide with his 59th birthday the following morning. The Japanese aerial assault on US positions in Guadalcanal and New Guinea would be the greatest since Pearl Harbor. Meanwhile, on Bougainville Island, returning pilots were reporting the destruction of an Allied cruiser and 25 transport ships, as well as over 200 Allied aircraft – the perfect belated birthday present for the Admiral. But Yamamoto was far from pleased. The news was too good to be true.

The Assassination of Admiral Yamamoto

The reality was that Yamamoto's aircraft had managed to sink the destroyer USS *Aaron Ward* and the corvette HMNZS *Moa* as well as the tanker USS *Kanawha*, but no cruisers were sunk and only seven Allied planes were lost against 21 Japanese. Yamamoto was right to be suspicious of his pilots' claims. His decision to visit them, at their Bougainville airfield in the Solomon Islands, however, would cost him his life.

The architect of the Pearl Harbor attack, Yamamoto was naturally a reviled figure in America and a key target for her military forces. Ironically, he had argued fiercely to his superiors that they should make peace with the US in 1940, as Japan could not hope to win a war. He was over-ruled and subsequently ordered to propose a strategy for a Japanese victory he never really believed was possible. Only then did he suggest that Japan should bomb Pearl Harbor, mindful that if the US was allowed to build up its strength it would rapidly acquire a navy that would dominate Japan's. From the outset, Yamamoto was attempting to find the least-worst option for his country.

In 1943, he was faced with the stark reality that Japanese forces, having been forced to withdraw from Guadalcanal, were now likely to lose the strategically important base of Rabaul unless a decisive blow could be struck against the Allies. Operation 'I-Go' was crucial to Yamamoto, and he was determined to be at the heart of the action to ensure success.

Operation Vengeance

Unknown to the Japanese Admiral, however, US Intelligence had cracked Japan's codes and was therefore able to listen in on the messages sent to the airfields on Bougainville Island. As the pilots of the Japanese air force prepared for the arrival of their illustrious guest, the pilots of the United States Army Air Force began to plan a very different reception for him. The name given to the mission betrayed the fact that this time it was personal ... Operation Vengeance.

To intercept the Japanese bomber carrying Yamamoto without being detected, USAAF fighter pilots needed to fly south and west of the Solomon Islands before surprising their target near Bougainville. It was a round-trip of 1,000 miles (1,600 km) – too far for

(Right) Lockheed P-38 Lightning.

THE SKIES OF THE PACIFIC

the Wildcats and Corsairs available to the Marines and Navy. Only US Army P-38G Lightnings could make the epic journey, and even these would need to be fitted with drop tanks.

The job was assigned to 339th Fighter Squadron, with 18 planes slated for the mission. Four would attack the formation carrying Yamamoto and the rest would provide top cover in the event of any Japanese fighter response. On their way to the kill-zone, they would fly at exceptionally low level and maintain radio silence throughout. Given the scarcity of fuel, the mission would require incredibly accurate timing. To succeed, the fighters needed to arrive in exactly the right place at exactly the right time.

Japanese Zero fighter plane wreck
at Papua New Guinea.

Closing in for The Kill

The Lightnings took off at 07:25 hours on the morning of 18 April 1943. Two immediately had to turn back – one due to a burst tyre and another due to a faulty drop tank. Around half an hour after the Americans took to the sky, Yamamoto climbed into the 'Betty' bomber which was scheduled to transport him from Rabaul, New Guinea to Bougainville Island in the Solomons. As usual, he was right on time, having ignored the pleas of local commanders to cancel the trip on the grounds of its danger. One other bomber and six Zero fighters escorted the Admiral. It was a small formation so as not to draw unwanted attention to itself.

For the next hour and a half, both groups of planes hurtled towards Bougainville Island from opposite directions until, at 09:34 hours, they came into contact. It was just one minute earlier than scheduled in the US plan. The Lightnings dropped their extra fuel tanks as soon as they spotted the Japanese formation flying close to the coastline of Bougainville. The 'kill group' of 339th Squadron moved towards their target while the others climbed to 18,000 ft (5,500 m) ready to cover them. Realizing the danger, the Zero fighters rushed to protect the bombers which banked hard to evade the incoming Lightnings.

Barber had gone with Lanphier on the initial attack. He went for one of the bombers but its maneuvers caused him to overshoot a little. He whipped back, however, and although pursued by Zeros, caught the bomber and destroyed it. When he fired, the tail section flew off, the bomber turned over on its back and plummeted to earth. By this time, Holmes had been able to drop his tank and with Hine, who had stayed in formation with him, came in toward the Zeros who were pursuing Barber. A dogfight ensued, many shots were exchanged, but results were not observed. The flight was on its way out of the combat area when Holmes noticed a stray bomber flying low over the water. He dove on it, his bursts getting it smoking in the left engine; Hine also shot at it and Barber polished it off with a burst in the fuselage.

US Army Intelligence summary describing the encounter in vivid detail.

Death of An Admiral

Yamamoto's body was found by a Japanese patrol that hacked through the jungle north of Buin on Bougainville Island the next day. His seat had been thrown clear of the wreckage of the plane and had landed beneath a tree. Yamamoto was sitting upright, with a white gloved hand resting on his samurai sword. He had a bullet hole just above his right eye.

A jubilant American public was told that civilian coast-watchers had tipped off the USAAF about Yamamoto's plane, so as not to betray the fact that the US had cracked Japan's codes. A shocked Japanese public was only officially told the news a month later. After the war, the pilots involved in the attack fought an acrimonious battle for the credit of shooting down Yamamoto's plane.

No matter who fired the deadly shots, however, Yamamoto's death resulted from an extraordinarily ambitious plan being executed with extreme precision. Its success stemmed from a combination of surprise and overwhelming force. Yamamoto's death was caused by the same lethal cocktail he himself had used to launch his most infamous attack in 1941.

LOCKHEED P-38 LIGHTNING

The Lockheed P-38 was a twin-engined fighter-bomber nicknamed 'Fork-Tailed Devil' by the Germans and 'Two planes one pilot' by the Japanese. Although the rate of roll was too slow for it to excel in dogfights, it remained a potent weapon and was the only American fighter aircraft to stay in production throughout World War II.

The brief Lockheed was following when designing the P-38 was for a plane having, 'the tactical mission of interception and attack of hostile aircraft at high altitude'. They took the unusual decision of using twin booms to accommodate the tail assembly, engines and turbo-superchargers. Few planes to date had looked at all like the P-38. Four Browning M2 machine guns and one Hispano 20mm cannon were all mounted in the nose, rather than on the wings, meaning that the P-38 required more accuracy from the gunner. The upside

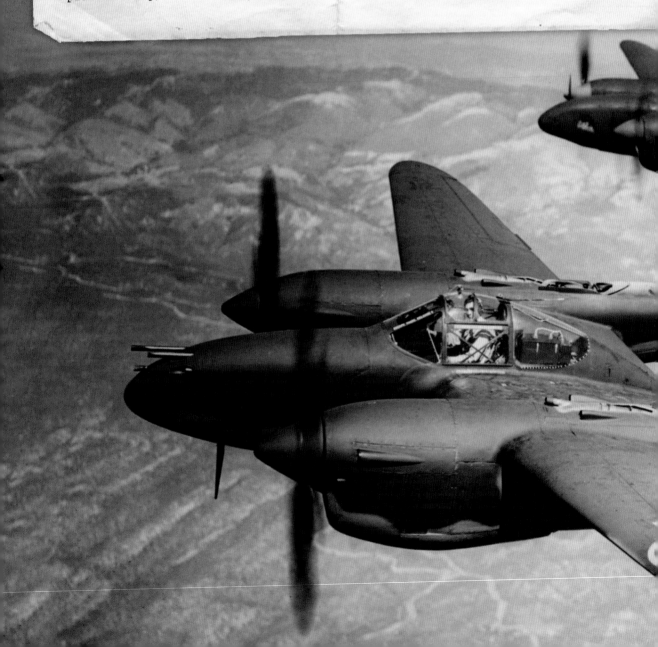

to the configuration was that a good pilot could travel much further due to the lack of a 'convergence zone' of fire. That certainly appealed to the likes of top US Aces Richard Bong and Thomas McGuire, who both scored heavily with the P-38.

The first P-38s were delivered to the USAAF in mid-1941, and 667 of the planes were ordered by the French and British. After the fall of France, the British took over the entire order and christened the P-38 'Lightning'. The RAF was displeased with the performance of the Mark I Lightnings and a bitter row broke out between the War Ministry and Lockheed, but the entry of the US into the war following the attack on Pearl Harbor thawed relations considerably. In truth the P-38's performance throughout the war was mixed — German fighters could easily escape the Lightning by diving away, but the plane's long range, ability to withstand punishment and ferocious firepower saw it account for 1,800 Japanese aircraft in the Pacific War. P-38s flew 130,000 sorties with a loss rate of 1.3%, comparable with the P-51 Mustang.

THE BATTLE OF THE ACES BONG V MCGUIRE

Richard I. Bong

The highest scoring USAAF Ace of all time, and recipient of the Medal of Honor, Richard Ira 'Dick' Bong was from a Swedish immigrant family in Wisconsin. After receiving his wings and a commission as second lieutenant, Bong first flew the twin-engined P-38 Lightning in 1942, and immediately fell in love with the plane. Indeed, he had so much fun in it that he was grounded just before his unit was sent to England to fight in the skies of Europe. Bong had been reprimanded for buzzing low over the house of a fellow pilot who had recently got married and — according to some accounts — for flying under the Golden Gate Bridge later on the same day. Once he had served his suspension he was sent not to Europe, but to the South West Pacific Area, which was to prove to be a most fruitful hunting ground.

Assigned to the 'Flying Knights' of 9th Fighter Squadron based at Darwin Australia, Bong flew missions with the 39th Fighter Squadron in order to gain combat experience. Flying out of Port Moresby, New Guinea, Bong scored his first victories of the war, during the Battle of Buna-Gona on 27 December 1942. Many more soon followed, including four kills in a single day in July 1943, an accomplishment that earned him the DSC to go with the Silver Star he had already, by then, acquired.

While on leave in November 1943, Bong met the love of his life, Marge Vattendahl, and from that moment on his P-38 proudly bore her name. Captain Bong and *Marge* soon surpassed Eddie Rickenbacker's all-time record of 26 confirmed kills, set in World War I. In the skies over New Guinea and the Philippines his tally rose to an extraordinary 40 victories before he was sent home to help promote the sale of war bonds in America in January 1945.

Ironically, perhaps, for such a prolific marksman, he considered himself a poor shot, and to compensate for this he tried to get as close as possible to his targets before firing. On several occasions he came close to colliding with his prey, and *Marge* was often scarred by debris blasted off enemy planes at close range. Bong was only 24 years old when he was killed whilst acting as a test pilot for the P-80 Shooting Star jet fighter in 1945. By this time he was so famous that news of his death managed to make the front page of national papers in the US despite it coinciding with the dropping of the first atomic bomb on Hiroshima.

Thomas B. McGuire

Thomas B. McGuire Jr. was highly competitive by nature, and became obsessed with taking Richard Bong's 'Ace of Aces' title from him towards the end of World War II. For much of the war McGuire had been just a few kills behind Bong, but when Bong was called home to be awarded his Medal of Honor, McGuire saw a chance to surpass his total. He rapidly progressed to 38 kills in the skies above New Guinea, before being suddenly grounded by General Kenney to ensure that the shine wasn't taken off Bong's achievements ahead of his medal presentation.

McGuire was back in action early in 1945, and desperate for the three kills that would take him past Bong's total. He was used to gaining easy kills with his P-38 against the Japanese 'Zero' fighters, and on 7 January he spotted what looked like a perfect target. A single Zero flying low over the jungle seemed too good a chance to miss, and so anxious was McGuire to add to his total that he neglected to disengage his drop tanks. In most circumstances his skill and accuracy would have seen him through, but on this occasion he faced a more formidable foe than he realized. Soichi Sugita was one of Japan's highest-scoring Aces with over 80 kills to his name. When the hunter became the hunted, McGuire crashed his P-38 and was killed.

Although McGuire remained tantalizing short of Bong's 40 kill total, he did receive the same recognition as Bong, albeit after his death. He was awarded a posthumous Medal of Honor for his astonishing bravery and skill.

Major Richard Bong (left) and Major Thomas McGuire (right) in the Philippines.

THE GREAT MARIANAS TURKEY SHOOT

DATELINE ... 19 JUNE 1944 ... 20 JUNE 1944

The new Commander-in-Chief of the Japanese Combined Fleet, Admiral Mineichi Koga, decided that it was time for Japan to return to the offensive in the Pacific. US forces had been making steady gains in the area, and their policy of 'island hopping' meant that another Pacific island invasion was highly likely in the near future. Koga hoped to attack the US fleet while it was attempting to support such an invasion. He reasoned that the ships would be 'pinned' by their support roles and thus more vulnerable to a massive counter-attack. As the Americans launched their amphibious assault on Saipan in the Mariana Islands on 12 June 1944, Koga authorized the operation which he hoped would shatter the US fleet and return the initiative to Japan.

Fury of the Hellcat

The Japanese fleet of five large aircraft carriers, four light carriers, five battleships and assorted cruisers and destroyers was commanded by Vice-Admiral Jisaburo Ozawa. Facing him was Admiral Raymond Spruance, the commander of the US 5th Fleet. Spruance's Task Force 58 was formed from five separate groups of ships. One consisted of seven fast battleships, another of three aircraft carriers and the rest of four carriers. These 'capital ships' were in turn protected by a range of destroyers, heavy and light cruisers, and submarines. Each fleet bristled with fighter planes – Mitsubishi

Zeroes in the case of the Japanese fleet, and the newly designed F6F Hellcats in the case of the US fleet.

Based on the earlier 'Wildcat', the F6F was specifically created after the experience of previous combat encounters with the Zeroes. The F6F's airframe was strengthened to allow it to incorporate a 2,000 hp Pratt & Whitney engine, resulting in a 25% increase in performance over the earlier Wildcat. The wings were low-mounted instead of mid-mounted and the cockpit was positioned high in the fuselage, providing much better all-round visibility for the pilot. The F6F also had a longer range than the Wildcat, while maintaining its ability to withstand far more damage than the lightly-built Zeroes.

The Battle of the Philippine Sea

A series of air attacks launched on the Mariana Islands on 12 June 1944 heralded the imminent invasion. The Japanese had only stationed 50 fighters there, expecting an American attack further to the south. The Japanese fleet moved into position to help defend the islands and launch their own counter-attack. It was sighted by the US fleet on 15 June, and from that moment on both sides knew that a major confrontation was looming. As the two fleets moved to establish the best possible attack position, the Americans had the advantage of having decrypted Japanese codes. They had a fix on

the Japanese flagship and by 18 June were within 350 miles (560 km). Close enough for the carrier planes to commence engagement.

Just after dawn on 19 June 1944, a Japanese air patrol sighted Task Force 58, radioed its position and attacked a destroyer before being shot down. The other 49 Zero fighters based on the island of Guam, were scrambled to intercept the fleet. But US Hellcats were already in the air and attacked them as they took off. An hour-long dogfight began during which 35 Zeroes were shot down before the Hellcats were recalled to their carriers. The reason for the recall was a worrying series of radar reports showing another large hostile fighter force heading for Task Force 58.

There were 68 Japanese Zeroes launched from her aircraft carriers. In response, Task Force 58 launched every fighter available. The Japanese planes circled to build an attack formation some 70 miles (110 km) from the US fleet. The time it took them to form up proved critical, giving the US fleet a chance to get a large number of Hellcats into the air. By the time the Zeroes had grouped themselves, the Americans were ready. Surprised by the sudden appearance of such a large enemy force, the Japanese fighters were overwhelmed and within a few minutes 25 had been shot down.

The remaining planes flew on to attack the USS *Yarnall* and USS *Stockham* but did little

(Above) US Navy Grumman F6F-3 *Hellcat* fighters on the flight deck of the aircraft carrier USS *Saratoga*, 1944.

damage. The USS *South Dakota* was hit and badly damaged, but further waves of Hellcats downed another 16 Zeroes in return. Just one Hellcat was lost in that first Japanese attack, and none of the Zeroes had managed to reach the US fleet's precious carriers. Vice-Admiral Ozawa, however, had only just begun and would not give up so easily.

The Great Marianas Turkey Shoot

A little after 11:00 hours, US radar detected another, much larger attack. This second wave consisted of 107 planes. The Zeroes were simply no match for the heavily armored and heavily armed Hellcats, however. The Americans intercepted the raiding party some 60 miles (95 km) from the fleet and scored so many successes against their enemy that this particular part of the Battle of the Philippine Sea became known as 'The Great Marianas Turkey Shoot'. At least 70 of the

> ## "... Hell, it was like an old time turkey shoot down home ..."
>
> US Pilot, USS Lexington

Japanese planes were shot down before they could reach the fleet. Six planes attacked the main carriers and caused casualties on two, but failed to put either out of action. In return, four of the six were blown out of the sky. Torpedo bombers attacked the USS *Enterprise* and USS *Princeton* but again failed to cause serious damage. The Japanese losses continued to mount at an alarming rate. Only 10 of the 107 planes of the second wave returned to base.

A third raid of 47 fighters followed shortly afterwards and was intercepted by 40 US fighters. This time many of the Japanese pilots failed to press home their attack, preferring instead to take evasive action. Nonetheless, a further seven planes were downed, and the US fleet remained essentially intact. A fourth raid lost their way after being given incorrect coordinates, but stumbled upon the American fleet while heading towards the island of Rota to refuel.

Once again the Hellcats were there to meet them, and nine more Japanese planes were destroyed.

Counting the Cost

Nine dive bombers did make it past the protective cover to attack the fleet, striking at the USS *Wasp* and USS *Bunker Hill*. But they scored no direct hits, and eight were gunned down during the attack. The rest of the fourth wave made an attempt to return to Guam, but were attacked by 27 Hellcats as they came into land. Of the 49 planes in this group, 30 were destroyed and the rest badly damaged.

By the end of the day, the Japanese had lost over 350 planes. The US had lost just 30 of its fighters and the damage to its fleet was minimal. Vice-Admiral Ozawa's air capability had been decimated in just a few hours. He didn't realize how serious the losses were, however, believing many of his planes had successfully landed in Guam. He ordered the fleet to remain in the area with the idea of launching a further attack. Before he could do so, US patrols found the Japanese fleet and a massive attack was launched against it.

The 226 US planes involved were met by just 35 Zero fighters. The carrier *Hiyo* was sunk by bombs and torpedos, and the carriers *Zuikaku*, *Junyo* and *Chiyoda* were all damaged, along with the battleship *Haruna*. American losses were light, at around 20 or so planes, but by the time the strike aircraft returned to their carriers darkness had fallen. It became desperately difficult to see the landing decks and many of the US pilots overshot or undershot on their approaches. A total of 80 planes crashed, the vast majority into the sea.

A Mortal Blow to the Empire

Ozawa immediately withdrew his shattered forces. Including submarine attacks he had lost three carriers as well as over 400 carrier aircraft. A further 200 land-based aircraft were also destroyed. US losses numbered 123 planes – the majority of which were lost to the disastrous night landings on the carrier decks. It was a mortal blow to the Imperial Japanese Navy. They no longer had the capacity to seriously challenge the US at sea. There were too few carriers remaining, and too few pilots to fly attack planes from those that did remain. The cream of Japan's naval fighter pilots were lost, and could not be replaced. Even worse, the Japanese now knew that the Americans possessed a deadly new fighter plane which outclassed the Zero. The F6F Hellcat dominated the skies over the Pacific for the rest of the war.

With the Japanese fleet taken out of the battle, US forces could concentrate on the battle for Saipan. On 20 June 1944 alone 11,536 tons of supplies were delivered, and the figure would steadily increase as more and more ships returned from their battle deployment areas. The Japanese garrison defending Saipan was doomed. The US took control of the island and thereby acquired a vital base from which to launch further attacks. The largest carrier-versus-carrier battle in history had resulted in a devastating defeat for the Japanese. The Empire of the Rising Sun was soon to discover just how costly the loss of the Mariana Islands would be. For now Japan itself was within range of US bombers.

(Left) P-47 US Thunderbolts taking off from Saipan in the Mariana Islands, 1944.

GRUMMAN F6F HELLCAT

The primary fighter of the United States Navy and Marine Corps in the second half of WWII, the F6F was responsible for more kills than any other Allied aircraft — 5,271 in total. Its design drew heavily on the lessons learned from aerial combat with the Japanese Zero fighter, which had shown itself to have a distinct edge over the earlier US F4F Wildcat. The Wildcat's advantages over the Zero — speed of dive and better armament — were retained, but the new plane was designed to have a much higher top speed and a longer range. A stronger airframe allowed a 2000 hp Pratt & Whitney R-2800 engine to be mounted, and the cockpit was redesigned to improve visibility. Self-sealing fuel tanks, bullet-resistant windshields and increased armour plating made the F6F less susceptible to enemy fire, and the ability to carry drop tanks increased its flying range.

The original rugged and easy to maintain design was so successful that few modifications were required during the war, increasing the rate of production. Over 11,000 were produced in just two years. The first Hellcats entered service on 1 September 1943 and proved an immediate success. By the end of the war the F6F had accounted for 75% of all aerial victories recorded by the US Navy in the Pacific, and 305 US Pilots achieved Ace status while flying a Hellcat.

My Girl, a P-51 Mustang, takes off from Iwo Jima, Pacific Ocean, 1945.

A Japanese aircraft crashes
into the Pacific after being
shot down at Saipan, 1945.

THE BOMBING OF HIROSHIMA AND NAGASAKI

DATELINE ... 6 AUGUST 1945 ... 15 AUGUST 1945

Having cracked Japan's code early in the war, US intelligence was able to listen to the Empire's reaction to the Potsdam Declaration of 26 July 1945. The ultimatum called for an immediate and unconditional Japanese surrender, and threatened 'inevitable and complete destruction' should they refuse. At the time Japan was effectively ruled by the Imperial Japanese Army General Hideki Tojo and while the man who was technically his senior, Emperor Hirohito, wanted an end to the war, Tojo was determined to fight on, though the situation appeared hopeless. For Tojo death was preferable to the shame and dishonour of unconditional surrender.

Suicide Attack Units

The US knew that although victory was now almost certain, an opposed invasion of Japan would cost many thousands of American lives. Since the autumn of 1944 they had witnessed first hand the fanaticism of the Japanese military. The experience of the US Naval fleet may well have influenced the decision of US High Command to attack Japan from the air rather than risk invasion. For they knew that Japan had for some months been stockpiling its own deadly new aerial weapon – the *Tsurugi*. It was a simple wooden plane with landing gear that could be dropped to the ground immediately after take-off. The planes had no need to land. They were the aircraft of the notorious *kamikaze* – the suicide attack units of the Empire of Japan

Tokyo Firebombing Campaign

Once the Mariana Islands fell into Allied hands, heavy bombing raids on Japan became possible for the first time. B-29 bombers flew from the islands from November 1944 onwards, and initially the targets were industrial facilities. However from March 1945, the USAAF increasingly directed its firepower against urban areas, and in June 1945 after the capture of Okinawa, a large Japanese island only 340 miles (550 km) from mainland Japan, the number of raids increased dramatically. A total of 67 Japanese cities were firebombed in the next six months, with the most devastating attack being on the capital city of Tokyo on 10 March 1945.

Operation Meetinghouse was the single most destructive bombing raid in history. Around 1,700 tons of bombs were dropped on Tokyo by 334 USAAF Boeing B-29 Superfortresses. The B-29, a propeller-driven, heavy strategic bomber used extensively in the low altitude fire bombing campaign of Japan, had been introduced in May 1944 as a successor to the B-17 Flying Fortress.

The majority of the bombs dropped by the B-29s were incendiaries, which turned the city's predominantly wooden buildings into a giant firestorm. An area of 16 square miles (42 square km) was completely consumed by the fire, and the number killed is estimated to have been around 100,000 people. At the time, Tokyo was the most densely populated city in the world, and it is believed over a million

THE DIVINE WIND OF THE KAMIKAZE

The first official *kamikaze* attack was carried out on 25 October 1944 during the Battle of Leyte Gulf. Earlier sporadic suicide attacks had been reported, but Vice-Admiral Takijirō Onishi's 'Special Attack Unit' was the first unit to adopt *kamikaze* as its primary tactic. By doing so, he hoped that what appeared to be a desperate situation for Japan could still be turned around. The first mission resulted in the carrier USS *St. Lo* being sunk by a *kamikaze*, and with the help of the suicidal pilots the Japanese managed to damage six other carriers and 40 other ships. Purpose-built *kamikaze* planes were soon produced, nicknamed 'Baka Bombs' (or 'Idiot Bombs') by the US forces. The planes were designed to be cheap and easy to manufacture, utilizing Japan's large stockpile of engines.

The Allies developed a defensive strategy called the 'big blue blanket', in which picket warships would patrol further out from the main fleet and radio the position of any enemy fighters they detected via radar. This gave time for Allied fighters to intercept them before they could reach the 'capital ships'. Late in 1944, the British Pacific Fleet used its Supermarine Seafires (a naval version of the Spitfire) to great effect against the *kamikazes*.

Known for its excellent high-altitude performance, the Seafire was able to swoop down and intercept the Japanese planes, and on a single day in August 1945 they destroyed eight while registering just one loss themselves.

The *kamikazes* tried to counter the Allies by launching in vast waves that could overwhelm the fighter cover, and the peak of their activity came in Operation Kikusui (Floating Chrysanthemums) during the Battle of Okinawa. Some 30 US warships were sunk or badly damaged, along with several merchant ships. However the attacks cost the Japanese 1,465 planes, and crucially in terms of the overall war, no carriers were sunk.

It is thought *kamikazes* sank between 30 and 60 ships and damaged hundreds of others, some of them beyond repair. Around 2,800 *kamikaze* pilots lost their lives, and they killed around 5,000 Allied sailors and wounded around the same number. The large number of Allied lives lost is what most concerned US High Command as their thoughts turned to the invasion of the Japanese homeland.

A Japanese Yokosuka D4Y3 *Kamikaze* in a suicide dive towards USS *Essex*, 1944.

citizens were left homeless by the attack. In addition, around half of Tokyo's industrial buildings were destroyed, crippling Japan's ability to manufacture the weapons it needed to continue the war.

Despite the unparalleled destruction witnessed in Tokyo, and the imminent threat of more such attacks, Japan decided to fight on. Future US air attacks were almost entirely unopposed as Japanese Army and Naval forces conserved their remaining fighters and ships in anticipation of the coming invasion of Japan.

The Americans, fearing a bloody struggle, decided to deploy the deadly secret nuclear weapon which had emerged from the 'Manhattan Project' in Los Alamos, New Mexico. No mention of the weapon had been made in the Potsdam Declaration, but the American threat of 'complete destruction' was about to be delivered by two atomic bombs which would stun the entire world.

Bombing Hiroshima

Hiroshima, a city near the south-western tip of Japan's largest island, Honshu, had a population of 350,000 people and was of major military and industrial significance. A key port of shipping and embarkation, Hiroshima was also the main base of the Japanese 2nd General Army and the Army Marine Headquarters. Crucially, in terms of testing the effects of the new atomic bomb, Hiroshima's adjacent hills were also likely to focus the blast and concentrate its effects, increasing the level of damage. Hiroshima was therefore selected as the primary target of the nuclear attack, with the cities of Nagasaki on the south-western coast of Kyushu island along

with the ancient town of Kokura on the Straits of Shimonoseki between Honshu and Kyushu, chosen as alternative targets should bad weather be encountered over Hiroshima.

On 6 August 1945, Colonel Paul W. Tibbets flew a B-29 Superfortress from the US airbase on Tinian Island in the Marianas and headed towards Japan. The *Enola Gay* was named after Tibbets' mother, and was accompanied by two other B-29s, *The Great Artiste* carrying instrumentation and the then unnamed *Necessary Evil* carrying reconnaissance equipment. The nuclear bomb carried by the *Enola Gay* was armed during the flight to reduce the risk of an explosion before or during take off. Code-named 'Little Boy', it was untested, as the enriched uranium used in its construction was in short supply. Tests had shown a plutonium bomb had worked, however, and the 'gun' type uranium bomb Little Boy was a relatively simple design. The safety devices on the bomb were removed 30 minutes before the *Enola Gay* reached its target. Visibility was clear over Hiroshima.

The blast was equivalent to 13 kilotons of TNT, and 4.7 square miles (12.2 square km) of the city was totally destroyed. Japanese officials later reported that almost 70% of Hiroshima's buildings were razed to the ground, and a further 7% damaged. The best estimate for those killed immediately is 70,000, with a further 70,000 injured. Burns, radiation and related diseases would increase the death toll to 90,000 by the end of 1945, with some estimates putting the figure as high as 166,000. Paul Tibbets later described the moment the bomb was released.

THE MAN WHO ENDED THE WAR
Paul Tibbets Jr.

Paul Tibbets was the pilot of the *Enola Gay*, the B-29 Superfortress that dropped the atomic bomb which led to the end of WWII. Tibbets was also recognized as the best flier in the US Army Air Force. After enlisting in 1937, as a lieutenant, he served as personal pilot to Brigadier General George S. Patton while stationed at Fort Benning. He was promoted to captain and trained to fly the Boeing B-17 Flying Fortress.

In 1942 he was deployed with the US 8th Air Force to England where he flew 25 bombing missions over France and Germany in Flying Fortresses based at RAF Polebrook. An experienced aviator, Tibbets was usually the choice to pilot top generals around Europe including the Supreme Allied Commander Lieutenant General Dwight D. Eisenhower himself. He was transferred to North Africa as part of James Doolittle's 12th Air Force and flew another 18 missions.

Doolittle recommended Tibbets as the ideal candidate, to help develop a new bomber — the B-29 Superfortress. So in 1943 he returned to America to work on the aircraft that would drop the atomic bomb. He was promoted to Colonel and put in command of the mission. On 6 August 1945, Tibbets and *Enola Gay*, took off from the Mariana Islands to fly the 2,000 miles (3,200 km) to Japan to drop the first atomic bomb in the history of military warfare.

On his return to America, he was celebrated as the man who brought the war to an end. But Tibbets never let fame go to his head and in 1975, he said in an interview, 'I'm not proud that I killed 80,000 people, but I'm proud that I was able to start with nothing, plan it and have it work as perfectly as it did … I sleep clearly every night.' Tibbets died in Columbus, Ohio, in 2007. He was 92 years old.

Colonel Paul Tibbets (center) with the crew of *Enola Gay*.

The devastated Japanese city of Hiroshima, in the aftermath of the atomic bomb, August 6, 1945.

THE SKIES OF THE PACIFIC

As soon as the weight had left the aeroplane I immediately went into this steep turn and we tried then to place distance between ourselves and the point of impact. In this particular case that bomb took 53 seconds from the time it left the aeroplane until it exploded and this gave us adequate time of course to make the turn. We had just made the turn and rolled out on level flight when it seemed like somebody had grabbed a hold of my aeroplane and gave it a real hard shaking because this was the shock wave that had come up ... I decided we'll turn around and go back and take a look ... Where before there had been a city with distinctive houses, buildings and everything you could see from our altitude, now you couldn't see anything except a black boiling debris down below.

Colonel Paul W. Tibbets, Pilot
USAAF B-29 Superfortress Enola Gay
6 August 1945

Aerial Apocalypse

The US President Harry S. Truman announced the use of the new weapon immediately after the attack and warned Japan that unless they surrendered they would face 'ruin from the air, the like of which has never been seen on this earth'. On 9 August 1945, the Soviet Union invaded the Japanese puppet state of Manchuria, and declared war on Japan, as agreed at the Yalta Conference. The Japanese Kwantung Army resisted fiercely but was rapidly overrun. Despite the massive invasion from the East and the devastation of Hiroshima delivered from the West, Japan refused to surrender.

On 9 August 1945, the US decided to drop a second atomic bomb, this time on the ancient castle city of Kokura. However, on the day in question, Kokura was wreathed in low cloud and the smoke from an earlier fire-

> **" ... We have discovered the most terrible bomb in the history of the world ..."**
>
> President Harry S. Truman, Diary Entry, 25 July 1945

bomb attack on the nearby city of Yahata. US bomber pilot Major Charles W. Sweeney headed instead for his secondary target. Meanwhile, on the island of Kyushu, a dull morning was brightening up into a beautiful day in the south-western seaport of Nagasaki.

Bombing Nagasaki

The B-29 tasked with delivering the second atomic bomb was the *Bockscar*, and the bomb in question was a plutonium nuclear device code-named 'Fat Man'. It had an explosive power equivalent to 21 kilotons of TNT. Major Sweeney had faced a number of problems on the flight: he had failed to rendezvous with the reconnaissance plane *Big Stink*, a transfer pump on his reserve fuel tank had failed and low cloud at Kokura meant he had to circle three times trying to spot his target.

Running dangerously low on fuel, the crew calculated they would have to divert to Okinawa as they could no longer make the intended return landing site of Iwo Jima. As they approached the secondary target of Nagasaki, they resolved that if low cloud prevented them seeing their target they would have to drop their bomb in the sea en route home. At 11:01 hours, a sudden short break in the cloud allowed them to release Fat Man. It exploded 43 seconds later, 1,500 ft (460 m) from the ground.

The bomb struck some 2 miles (3 km) from the intended target, and as a result a large part of the city was protected from the worst of the blast by hills. Nonetheless, a 624mph and 3,900 degrees Celsius blast wave tore through the Urakami Valley.

(Right) Atomic explosion, Hiroshima, 1945.

Between 40,000 and 75,000 people were killed instantly, and the final death toll is believed to have exceeded 80,000. Thousands of houses and commercial buildings were also destroyed, among them the Mitsubishi-Urakami Ordnance Works – the factory that produced the torpedoes that devastated the US Fleet at Pearl Harbor.

Japan's Unsufferable Surrender

Emperor Hirohito's *Gyokuon-hoso* ('Jewel Voice Broadcast') was delivered to the Japanese people by radio broadcast on 15 August 1945, announcing that the Japanese Government had accepted the Potsdam Declaration.

The Japanese people had never heard their Emperor speak before, and the poor quality of the phonograph recording, combined with his courtly language, made the broadcast difficult to understand. So, immediately after the broadcast a radio announcer clarified what had happened. Japan had surrendered unconditionally. World War II was over.

It is according to the dictates of time and fate that we have resolved to pave the way for a grand peace for all the generations to come by enduring the unendurable and suffering what is unsufferable.

Emperor Showa, Hirohito, 124th Emperor of Japan
Surrender Speech, 15 August 1945

BOEING B-29 SUPERFORTRESS

An American four-engined heavy bomber, the Boeing B-29 Superfortress was flown in the final years of the war with Japan and was responsible for the atomic bomb attacks on Hiroshima and Nagasaki. At the end of WWII, many other bombers were decommissioned immediately, but B-29s remained in service long after the war and were deployed during bombing raids in the Korean War of 1950 — 53, finally retiring in 1960.

One of the largest bombers of the era, the on-board technology was amazingly advanced for an aircraft of that time, including a pressurized cabin and remote controlled gun turrets. Taking its name from its famous Boeing predecessor, the Flying Fortress, the Superfortress was originally designed as a high altitude strategic bomber. However, B-29s performed so well at low levels that they became indispensable during the USAAF's firebombing and night time incendiary bombing campaigns of Japan.

POSTSCRIPT

In the United States and Great Britain, the euphoria of victory soon turned into a demand to 'Bring the boys home for Christmas'. One of the most extraordinary sealift operations in history was launched to do just that. Operation Magic Carpet saw over 4.5 million American service personnel brought back within 12 months, with the vast majority of them able to celebrate Christmas 1945 at home. The Army's Air Transport Command flew thousands of sorties during the operation and the aircraft carrier USS *Lake Champlain* became a make-shift troop carrier. Magic Carpet was one of the greatest mass transportation operations ever undertaken.

Charlie Brown and the Franz Stigler Incident

One of those who felt especially relieved to be returning home was USAAF Second Lieutenant Charles L. Brown. His story serves as a reminder of the million human triumphs and tragedies that lie behind the bare statistics of the war. Brown took off from Kimbolton in southern England on a mission to attack an aircraft factory in Bremen, Germany. It was five days before Christmas in 1943.

Brown's B-17 Flying Fortress, *Ye Olde Pub*, was hammered by flak on the approach and then attacked by eight German fighters. One engine was destroyed and two others damaged, and the plane's nose was blown off. The rear gunner was killed and the rest of the crew were badly injured, including Brown himself, who blacked out at one point but regained consciousness in time to haul his crippled bomber away from the ground. Flying at tree-top level, Brown's 'heart sank' as he passed directly over a German airfield, where Luftwaffe pilot Franz Stigler was re-fuelling his Messerschmitt Bf 109 after an earlier mission. Stigler was an experienced pilot who had already downed two Allied bombers that day. He jumped into his fighter and pursued *Ye Olde Pub*, rapidly catching up with the stricken B-17.

As Stigler approached he was conscious of the lack of defensive fire being put out by the Allied plane, and as he drew closer he could easily ascertain the reason. *Ye Olde Pub* was a mess. Huge holes had been punched through the fuselage of the bomber, and through them Stigler watched the bleeding crew members desperately try and help one another. He flew alongside and signalled to Brown that he should land at the nearest German airbase, but Brown refused and continued to limp for home.

What followed is the only documented case of its kind: the Allies' most destructive bomber being escorted to safety by the Luftwaffe's most deadly fighter. Stigler elected not to shoot down Brown's plane, but instead flew alongside it across Occupied Europe and out into the North Sea. When he was sure the bomber was safe from attack, Stigler saluted to Brown, rolled his plane away and flew back to his base. Brown nursed his plane back to England and landed safely, saving the lives of the rest of his crew.

All wars dehumanize, and World War II was the first war fought with machines that could bring death to tens of thousands at the flick of a switch. Yet the story of Stigler and Brown reminds us that often the combatants bore one another no personal grudge, and that even amidst slaughter on an industrial scale, human beings are capable of small acts of mercy. The two pilots were reunited after the war and became firm friends, seeing one another regularly until their deaths in 2008.

Franz Stigler explained away his act of chivalry by referring to his commander's words to him when on active service in North Africa: 'If I ever hear of any of you shooting at someone in a parachute, I'll shoot you myself. You are fighter pilots first, last, always.'

Onboard USS *Boise*, Private Felix Uva (left) and Corporal Donald Purdy are going home to the United States from Europe in November 1945, after World War II had ended.

Brand new B-25 Mitchell bombers ready for war, at North American Aviation Incorporated, Kansas City, Kansas, 1942.

INDEX

Picture Credits

Inspiring | Educating | Creating | Entertaining

Brimming with creative inspiration, how-to projects, and useful information to enrich your everyday life, Quarto Knows is a favorite destination for those pursuing their interests and passions. Visit our site and dig deeper with our books into your area of interest: Quarto Creates, Quarto Cooks, Quarto Homes, Quarto Lives, Quarto Drives, Quarto Explores, Quarto Gifts, or Quarto Kids.

© 2014 Oxford Publishing Ventures Ltd.

This edition published in 2014 by Chartwell Books, an imprint of The Quarto Group, 142 West 36th Street, 4th Floor, New York, NY 10018, USA
T (212) 779-4972 F (212) 779-6058
www.QuartoKnows.com

Chartwell Books titles are also available at discount for retail, wholesale, promotional, and bulk purchase. For details, contact the Special Sales Manager by email at specialsales@ quarto.com or by mail at The Quarto Group, Attn: Special Sales Manager, 401 Second Avenue North, Suite 310, Minneapolis, MN 55401, USA.

10 9 8 7 6 5 4 3 2

ISBN: 978-0-7858-3111-2

Printed in China